AD/HD Teens:
Distracted or Defiant?

AD/HD Teens: Distracted or Defiant?

✦

Coaching Helps!

Coaching Strategies for
Adolescents, Parents, Teachers and Coaches

Joyce Walker, MCC
Master Certified Coach

Question and Answers Section Included

iUniverse, Inc.
New York Lincoln Shanghai

AD/HD Teens: Distracted or Defiant?
Coaching Helps!

Copyright © 2006 by Joyce Walker

iUniverse books may be ordered through booksellers or by contacting:

iUniverse
2021 Pine Lake Road, Suite 100
Lincoln, NE 68512
www.iuniverse.com
1-800-Authors (1-800-288-4677)

ISBN-13: 978-0-595-37038-2 (pbk)
ISBN-13: 978-0-595-81442-8 (ebk)
ISBN-10: 0-595-37038-1 (pbk)
ISBN-10: 0-595-81442-5 (ebk)

Printed in the United States of America

NOTES FROM THE AUTHOR

AD/HD is the DSM-IV abbreviation for **Attention Deficit Hyperactivity Disorder**, previously referred to as **ADD**. It is often called simply **Attention Deficit Disorder.** Any of the above terms are used to include all aspects of the disorder, both hyperactive and inattentive (non-hyperactive) types. To underscore the fact that observable hyperactivity is not present in everyone with the disorder, ADD and AD/HD are used interchangeably in this book. **ADHD** will sometimes be used to refer to the hyperactive type specifically.

Throughout this book I frequently used the word ADDer. This word refers to someone who has AD/HD.

The material presented in this book is intended for informational purposes only and should never be considered a substitute for psychological or medical advice. If you do not agree with some of the information or answers to the questions, please remember that the work was done from an individual ADD coach's viewpoint, experience and research.

I am not a physician; I am a Master Certified Coach, (MCC) with a passion for helping people. I have several years of ADD—specific training and many years of experience working with ADD clients. I would especially like to thank my past and present teen clients for giving me the coaching experience along with the opportunity of helping them to achieve their goals and overcome their challenges.

As I created this book, I used my experience in my coaching practice along with my coach training knowledge and, with permission, information from my coach training materials. I have made every attempt to present the information I have gathered from numerous professional resources as accurately as possible.

This book is one of a few books in circulation dealing with coaching teens and I believe it fills a void. Sit back, elevate your feet, and begin reading a book long needed to help teens and the people associated with them. I hope that you enjoy reading my book, with the enthusiasm with which I created it and that you have a wonderful reading experience!

This book is dedicated to my late mother and father, Martha and Seymour Dickman. I miss my parents enormously and am grateful that I had them for as long as I did. I have deep gratitude and respect for my parents. I was raised with lots of love and support. My parents gave me my values, ethics and honesty and taught me right from wrong. I continue to value the lessons I learned as a child and have endeavored to impart those lessons to my children and the people I coach.

Contents

Acknowledgements

I find myself approaching this section with great fear that I will forget to acknowledge someone. If I do so, please forgive me.

First of all, I dearly thank Madelyn Griffith-Haynie, better known as MGH. Without her personal coaching, her marvelous ADD-focused coach-training program and the company she founded, The Optimal Functioning Institute™, this book would not exist. MGH helped me change from an insecure, dependent person to a confident, independent woman with tremendous self-esteem.

Next, I wish to thank all of my teenage clients[1], past and present. They have taught me almost as much as I have taught them. To see their personal, emotional, psychological, social and educational growth has been so rewarding to me, and form the basis of much of the information contained in this book. I love and respect them all.

I especially want to thank several of my teen clients who have actively participated in the creation of this book. *Jeff*, 15, did an excellent job typing several chapters for me. *Tom*, 17, did a splendid job with an essay about how coaching helped him, generously allowing me to use it in this book, along with one of his coaching situations. *Jerico*, 16, also gave me permission to use one of his situations.

I also want to thank my psychiatrist who prescribes and monitors my medication, which enables me to function as well as I do.

My husband Ray and daughters Kim and Heather have been very patient and supportive of me. They have also been an inspiration. I send them all much love and respect.

---

1.   The *names* of all clients in this book have been changed to protect their privacy.

Preface

There is a lot of information I included for background to the coaching suggestions in *AD/HD Teens: Distracted or Defiant?,* to help the reader understand what is going on with ADD and how it can create struggles with the tasks of life, especially for teens.

I included the chapter on **Neurology and Parts of the Brain** to help the reader understand the dynamics of AD/HD and the co-existing conditions that often accompany it.

I was extremely interested in the functions of the different parts of the brain personally when I began to learn about my own ADD. I now believe that knowing about brain parts, functions and abnormalities are essential expects to understand how and why co-existing conditions may occur that can complicate symptoms, challenges and potential solutions.

It is *essential* for a teenager who has a disability like ADD to understand the disorder that has such a great influence on the teen him or herself: the teen's social life and success in school, as well as on the teen's family and close relationships.

To look forward to experiencing all that life has to offer, it is very important for teens to understand the specific impact of their own ADD presentations in addition to AD/HD overall.

A well-trained ADD coach can assist anyone in determining how AD/HD affects life and what needs to be done to treat, accommodate, and compensate for ADD challenges and problems. Without the awareness and assistance from a coach who understands ADD, learning dynamics and teens, however, AD/HD may prevent the teen from reaching his or her full potential as an adult.

It is important for those who work with teens to be aware of the different ways people learn so that teens with AD/HD aren't slipping between the cracks. The section on modalities is critical to teens and the people trying to help them.

In addition to specific ADD information an ADD Coach must be able to provide, AD/HD coaching is involved with everyday living and the practical matters of life. Time management, organizational skills, memory problems, procrastination, and any other functional challenges are dealt with in ADD coaching. An ADD Coach helps a teen create goals and an action plan, and makes sure the teen follows through the simplest way possible, enabling them teen to accomplish without frustration.

A coach will keep the teen involved in the process by asking pertinent questions to stimulate his brain. With a coach's knowledge of strategies, structure, interventions, solutions and systems, coupled with the use of medication if warranted, a teen is given the opportunity to become highly successful.

Author's Introduction

My name is Joyce Walker and I am a high functioning adult with ADD, Attention Deficit Disorder. I am also an ADD Coach, a "Personal & Professional Life Coach" in private practice with special focus on AD/HD and Entrepreneurial coaching. I was initially diagnosed with ADD at the age of 45 while taking a course called the "Human Potential Seminar." As one student gave an oral presentation of a book she read, my eyes widened and my jaw dropped. It sounded like my autobiography.

The book she was discussing was called *Driven to Distraction* by Dr. John Ratey and Dr. Edward Hallowell, both of whom have AD/HD. I bought the book practically immediately, and within weeks I found a psychiatrist specializing in diagnosing and treating AD/HD. After he diagnosed me with Inattentive ADD, I was given a prescription for medication.

While I was being evaluated, I became aware for the first time of the impact of ADD on my childhood. The psychiatrist had me fill out several questionnaires regarding family, school, personal and medical history and my challenges and functioning. These questions brought back many childhood memories.

My mother told me she would often sit me on a blanket and hand me a flower. I would stare at it for hours. Perhaps I was daydreaming even then, and maybe now some of those dreams are coming true. My mother, may she rest in peace, commented only that I was "such a good baby."

Throughout my years in school, I was teased by other children for "odd" behavior, yelled at by teachers for my lack of attention, and always made to feel different.

In kindergarten I was teased and laughed at while playing in the sandbox when I would simply sit and pour the sand back and forth. During story time, the teacher would yell at me for looking out the window instead of listening attentively with eyes focused on her.

Once, in first grade, I was talking to a classmate instead of paying attention to what the teacher was saying. My teacher stopped class, grabbed my hand and made me walk with her to each desk and say hello to each child.

I was fooling around in high school French class one day and bumped my elbow so hard I fainted. My teacher had to pick me up off the floor.

On my report cards from elementary through high school, there were comments like, *"Doesn't work up to ability," "Doesn't try hard enough," "Doesn't pay attention,"* and *"Doesn't do well on tests."* Even private tutoring didn't seem to help. No one could understand why I had such difficult time learning, studying and doing homework assignments.

With a lot of determination, I was able to graduate from high school and college and to become a nurse. I worked as a pediatric nurse until my own children were born. I later worked part-time in marketing and sales while my children were in school. I also taught at local schools as a Teaching Assistant. I always had the feeling I had to work a lot harder than others with my level of intelligence to accomplish my goals, but I never understood why until I was diagnosed with ADD.

After my diagnosis I began my search for an adult ADD coach.

One of the first references to ADD coaching is on page 226 of my copy of *Driven to Distraction*. Many people have sought coaches to help their ADD children's development as a result of this reference. Even more, I hope, will be inspired to reach out for coaching help as the result of my book.

I was extremely fortunate to find an enthusiastic and knowledgeable coach, Madelyn Griffith-Haynie. Known as MGH to her clients, students and many of her colleagues, she has not only been a coach and role model for me but has helped me do the same for others.

I was inspired to write a poem about my experience dedicated to MGH which I decided not to include in this book, but I will be happy to send it to you by email. You will find my email address at the end of this book.

MGH founded The Optimal Functioning Institute™ [OFI], a virtual ADD and systems-development coach-training company, developed the first international coaching clinic as well as the ADD Coach Training program where I received my training. OFI's A.C.T. Program was the only comprehensive ADD-specific coach training program in the world for several years, and is still the most comprehensive. The OFI website is www.addcoach.com.

I graduated from Optimal Functioning Institute's (OFI's) A.C.T. Program in 1996 and received my Master Coach Certification from the International Coach Federation [ICF] in 1999 with the first group of coaches to attain certification. Master Certified Coach, MCC is the highest level of certification awarded by ICF, the professional association of personal and business coaches.

ICF seeks to preserve the integrity of coaching around the world through the certification process. ICF also has an international coach referral system to help people find coaches.

I recently accepted an invitation to become a member at the Accreditation Committee of the IAAC, the institute for achievement of AD/HD coaches. Their primary goal is to develop an international accreditations process for certification of AD/HD coaches.

The Purpose of My Book

The main purpose of my book is to educate AD/HD teenagers, their patents, coaches and anyone working with ADD teens about what ADD coaching is and what it can accomplish.

In order to show how helpful coaching can be, I've included background information about AD/HD (including neurological involvement), as well as some background on the co-existing conditions that may accompany it. The reader will learn about the major challenges ADD presents, and how ADD can be managed and turned into an advantage. Many examples of coaching are presented to give the reader an understanding of how coaching works.

ADD Coaching is a powerful instrument and comes with its own set of tools, structure and support. It creates a positive relationship that promotes growth and independence for AD/HD teens.

An ADD coach is non-judgmental: the goal of ADD coaching is to provide support to help clients to form good habits, develop structure, and implement systems for success, regardless of the number of functional challenges at the onset. With proper coaching, teens will begin to focus on developing and improving their abilities, their self esteem will increase as a result, and they will believe they will be able to achieve any goal they are willing to work toward.

There are many specialties of coaches. I am an AD/HD Systems Development Coach, and my specialty is assisting teens to achieve their goals by learning how to break tasks down into manageable steps to conquer these goals one step at a time.

Coaching is an enormously fulfilling and exciting profession and I love motivating AD/HD teens and encouraging them to discover their gifts. I rarely turn teens away, especially since they often come to me as a last resort. I use every tool I have to get through to them and earn their respect and trust. I coach teens from my heart, soul and gut.

ADD Coaching can be time-consuming and energy draining, but the rewards are worth it. Fortunately, the motivated teens and dedicated parents who seek coaching make a coach's job easier.

Another purpose of this book is to give the reader an understanding of AD/HD.

Whether diagnosed or not, ADD teens have been laughed at, called trouble-makers, stupid, lazy, daydreamers or underachievers at some part of their life. They appear different, often lack social skills, have difficulty remembering things and can't always express themselves or control their behavior.

All adolescents deserve to be treated with love and respect so that they can fulfill their potential as intelligent, interesting, creative, emotional, resourceful, and caring individuals—especially the ones who are struggling.

1

What is AD/HD?

Attention Deficit Hyperactivity Disorder refers to a family of disorders marked by attentional impairment, disorganization, distractibility, impulsivity, motor hyperactivity or hypo activity, low frustration tolerance, time management issues, procrastination, incompletion and conduct problems.

Many doctors and researchers believe that AD/HD is a neurological and biochemical disorder. They believe that ADD affects and impairs behavior and learning, including short-term memory, attention capacity, impulsiveness, time management, decision-making, prioritizing, completion, procrastination, and transitions.

ADD is primarily transmitted genetically and numerous genes are involved. It is believed to be caused by a chemical imbalance in the brain, such as too much or too little dopamine, epinephrine, or serotonin. Some parts of the brain may be over active while others are under active.

ADD is neurobiologically based and can be treated by medication, which should be administered in conjunction with therapy, education about the disorder and coaching. Unless the appropriate medications are taken, however, other treatment methods often don't work.

Though no one necessarily has all of them, the following characteristics are frequently found in teens with Attention Deficit Disorder:

- History of difficulty in school in both the learning and behavior areas
- Failing classes or being left back
- Difficulty and awkwardness in peer relationships
- Tendency to be accident prone or clumsy
- Failure to perform up to ability

- Poor response to discipline
- Emotional sensitivity
- High tolerance to pain
- Difficulty getting started, especially in the morning
- Difficulty getting to sleep at night and getting up in the morning
- "Violent" sleeping patterns, bedwetting, sleepwalking or sleep talking
- Poor organizational skills
- Seeking of highly stimulating environments
- Passivity

Teens with Inattentive ADD, though often socially immature, are usually well behaved in class. They are frequently late to school or class, have difficulty concentrating and are forgetful. Because they are not troublemakers, they sometimes fall "between the cracks" and are never diagnosed.

Girls with ADD tend to suffer from this type of ADD more often than boys and are often not diagnosed as a result. Inattentive ADD is often very responsive to stimulant medication.

Teens with Inattentive ADD show symptoms of

- Inattentiveness
- Chronic boredom
- Decreased motivation
- Internal preoccupation, and
- Low energy.

Lisa

In a typical scenario, "Lisa" runs into class two minutes after the bell rings. Lisa is chronically late, doesn't know the answer when called upon, and is usually staring out the window when other students are taking notes or paying attention to the teacher.

Her teacher thinks she is unreliable, lazy and an underachiever. It is very possible that Lisa has undiagnosed Inattentive ADD.

Teens with ADHD, the type of Attention Deficit Disorder that includes observable Hyperactivity, exhibit physical and mental restlessness, are easily distractible and have difficulty focusing on intended stimuli. This form of ADD is usually very noticeable.

The teen with ADHD may seem like an uncontrollable tornado: not able to sit still or stop talking, misbehaving in class, and unable to follow directions. A teen with ADHD may be the "class clown."

Some of the challenges of ADHD are:

- Difficulty resuming activity after it has stopped

- Difficulty shifting gears

- Disorganization and

- Social awkwardness.

Co-existing disorders

A total treatment program is essential if the teen expects to fulfill his or her potential. It is common to have other symptoms or disorders with ADD, which are referred to as co-existing conditions or co-morbidity. This term co-morbidity is often used regardless of whether the additional symptoms co-exist with AD/HD as an independent diagnosis or appear as a result of reaction to ADD symptoms.

Co-existing disorders that frequently appear with AD/HD are:

- Learning disorders

- Sleep disorders—chronic insomnia, narcolepsy and difficulty awakening

- Anxiety

- Aggression

- Hyper-reactivity

- Depression

- Addictive disorders

- Substance abuse

- Obsessive-compulsive disorder (OCD)

- Bi-polar disorders

- Behavioral disorders—oppositional deficit disorder, conduct disorder

- Auditory perception problems

- Autism

- Asperser's syndrome

- Tourette's syndrome

Understanding how the human brain functions is a mystery that researchers have been trying to solve for centuries. Today, neuroscientists and ADD specialists are exploring the brain more than ever before. Discoveries in neuroscience are soaring, and information about these discoveries is publicized in newspapers, magazines, medical journals, and even on television talk shows.

It can be difficult to find an experienced physician who is continuously educated about the recent ADD research, treatments, medications and co-existing conditions.

Even with an-up-to-the-minute psychiatrist or neurologist, it may be difficult to arrive at the proper medications, dosage, or combination of medications.

The earlier one is properly diagnosed, the sooner treatment can begin. Research has concluded that treatment is the most effective when a multi-model approach is used. This is a combination of counseling, medication, coaching and education.

SPECT Imaging

SPECT Imaging is a nuclear medicine technique that evaluates brain blood flow and activity patterns. Through these images, we now have visual evidence of brain patterns that correlate with behavior.

SPECT stands for "single photon emission computed 3-D picture tomography." It captures a picture of cerebral blood fluids (an indirect measure of brain metabolism). Using SPECT studies, doctors are able to more effectively pinpoint troubled areas of the brain and provide more appropriate interventions.

Dr. Daniel Amen is one of the country's foremost pioneers in applying SPECT Imaging science to clinical practice, especially in the area of ADD. In his books, *Change Your Brain, Change Your Life* and *Healing ADD,* Dr. Amen presents a variety of photos of ADD and non-ADD SPECT brain scans. Through these scans, Dr. Amen came to the conclusion that when attempting to focus on a task or respond to an intellectual challenge, people with ADD experience different levels of activity in their brains than do people without ADD.

Dr. Amen states:

"These images make it plain that many problems long thought to be psychiatric in nature—depression, panic attacks, deficit disorders—are actually medical problems that can be treated using a medical model along with traditional psychological and sociological models."

The following section was based on information in *Healing ADD* by Dr. Daniel Amen.

The ADD Brain

The Prefrontal Cortex is considered to be the supervisory and executive functioning part of the brain. It is located at the front tip of the brain, right behind the forehead.

The prefrontal cortex controls focusing as well as other functions. It produces adrenaline, a neurotransmitter which stimulates the brain but can inhibit action. Adrenaline can create anxiety or fear, which can produce immobilization as well as the "fight or flight" response.

It is believed that people with attentional challenges have a neurotransmitter imbalance that affects the brain's Prefrontal Cortex particularly.

- While the brains of people without ADD show *increased* prefrontal cortex activity when asked to perform, the prefrontal cortex of an ADDer asked to perform the same activity may actually "shut down" for an instant first; there is an immediate observable *decrease* in prefrontal cortex activity.

- People with Inattentive ADD show decreased activity in the prefrontal cortex when attempting to focus or concentrate.

The following are some of the major functions of the prefrontal cortex:

- Feeling and expression of emotions
- Day-to-day organization of life

- Concentration

- Attention span

- Judgment

- Impulse control

- Planning ahead

- Communication with others

- Conscious thought

- Critical thinking

If there is decreased activity in the prefrontal cortex, people will have cognitive difficulty. Schizophrenia and clinical depression are extreme examples of cognitive difficulties that have a neurobiological cause similar to the one that produces ADD.

Other Parts of the Brain

Introduced briefly below are other areas of the brain implicated in ADD. These areas will be explored more thoroughly in the next chapter.

The Basal Ganglia stores patterns of learned behavior and programming of the past and sets the body's anxiety level. It is the processing center and it controls functions critical to human behavior. It is also where negative patterns of behavior are stored.

The Cingulate Gyrus allows you to shift attention from one thing to another, to move from one idea to another and to see options in life. Abnormalities include difficulty in shifting of thoughts, inappropriate amount of neurochemicals, and Obsessive Compulsive Disorder (OCD).

The Limbic System sets a person's emotional tone and stores highly charged memories, both positive and negative.

The Temporal Lobes are involved with memory, learning, experiences, and language. Abnormalities of the temporal lobe can cause anxiety, irritability, anger, rage, depression and social withdrawal.

Neurotransmitters

Neurotransmitters are the chemical messengers between neurons—how the various parts of the human brain coordinate with one another. ADD Medications are prescribed to increase the amount of specific neurotransmitters available for the brain to do its work, referred to as increasing neurotransmitter *bio availability*. The neurotransmitters that are generally agreed to be important for the areas of day-to-day functioning that seem to be difficult for ADDers are listed below:

Serotonin is an inhibitory neurotransmitter (probably controlled by the light/dark cycle); it is believed to produce sleep. It is probably a neurohormone (acting on overall brain functioning and mood settings).

Dopamine (DA) controls movement. Parkinson's disease is a result of the death of cells in dopamine-producing centers (deep in the brain base).

Epinephrine (EPI) is better known as *adrenaline*. It is the mobilizing neurotransmitter that produces the "fight-or-flight" response in reaction to danger where the pupils dilate, the heart beats faster and the breathing passages become wider.

Norepinephrine (NE) is produced by the adrenal glands. It acts as a stimulant to both the body and the brain. Also secreted by a small group of cells located in the brain stem that connect with most of the rest of the brain, it has adrenaline-like effect on brain capillaries and some nerve cells, increasing blood flow and arousing nerve cells in a stimulant fashion.

Endorphins are positive transmitters are known as "natural morphine." They give you a feeling of success. Endorphins calm and relieve stress, and reduce awareness of pain and irritation. They can be produced by exercise.

Monoamine Oxidase (MAO) is the enzyme that breaks serotonin, dopamine and norepinephrine into smaller particles.

2

Neurology and Parts of the Brain

Understanding what makes the brain tick is helpful in understanding ADD and Learning Disabilities.

Researchers like Dr. Daniel Amen, H. Joseph Horace and David Comings have studied the cause, effect, and treatment of ADD people for years. As a result to their ideas and research on ADD., there is now new hope for people with ADD and its co-occurring conditions.

Thanks to their efforts, we have proof that many behaviors are neurobiological driven, caused by a difference in the genetic pattern of those who exhibit them, and that Attention Deficit Disorder is a genetically caused disorder with several genes involved.

The importance of SPECT research

Dr. Daniel Amen, the ADD doctor who has done extensive SPECT research on the brain, has compared the ADD brain and the non-ADD brain using that special kind of brain scan. You can see a remarkable difference between the two in the pictures that result.

AD/HD combined type or predominantly hyperactive-impulsive type is often identified early in life, especially in boys. The level of hyperactivity, restlessness, and impulsivity causes them to stand out from others.

The earlier one is properly diagnosed; the sooner treatment can begin, including a combination of medication, counseling, coaching and education.

The promise of SPECT research and functional brain scans is that we will some day have a way to identify all ADDers early in life.

How they work

Dr. Amen's pictures are created by what is called a functional brain scan, in contrast to earlier brain scans which could only take pictures of that static brain. Functional brain scans can take a picture of a working brain, a result of advances in nuclear medicine technology.

A small amount of radioactive substance is injected into an individual so that the brain's metabolism can be measured. by special cameras designed to be sensitive to the substance injected. The pictures are put together and made clearer with the use of computer technology.

What they show

It has long been believed by researchers that different parts of the brain control different things and Dr. Amen's image research seem to support that belief.

Through SPECT scans of the ADHD brain, Dr. Amen came to the conclusion that when attempting to focus or concentrate on a task, such people experience decreased activity in their pre-frontal cortex.

The pre-frontal cortex is considered to be the supervision and executive functioning portion of the brain. Since Attention is regulated from that area, it is believed that people with attention issues have a neurotransmitter imbalance that is particular evident in the pre-frontal cortex.

Adrenaline (epinephrine) is a stimulating neurotransmitter that can seem to inhibit focused control.

I'm sure you have heard the expression "fight or flight." That reaction is produced by adrenaline. The effect of too much or too little adrenaline production can also create anxiety, fear, and immobilization. If you have too little adrenaline, you will lack focus and have interruptions in the thought process.

Focusing on logic can slow down the production of adrenaline. Beta waves, produced in states of focused concentration, can counteract hyper-focusing (over-concentration) and hypo-focusing (daydreaming).

- If you tend to hyper focus on negative thoughts, which the ADD field calls *rumination*, you may be producing too much adrenaline.

- Focusing on positive thoughts create serotonin, an inhibitory neurotransmitter that counteracts an escalating focus on negative thoughts, created by adrenaline.

Comorbidity

Comorbidity means that one or more emotional/mental disorders are often found at the same time as a primary diagnosis, to a degree statistically greater than their occurrence in the general population.

ADD can be found with co-morbid conditions such as anxiety and mood disorders, learning disabilities, obsessive-compulsive disorder, oppositional disorder, rage disorder, conduct disorder, addictive illness (alcohol, drugs gambling, sex, and food) depression, and Tourette's Syndrome.

Each of those disorders produce can be identified by their own particular patterns of neurotransmitter activity in particular areas of the brain.

Brain Functions of the Parts of the Brain

According to various brain researchers like Daniel Amen, parts of the brain have regulatory responsibility for different brain functions and abnormalities. Since ADD is often accompanied by other disorders, I thought this information would be interesting and informative.

The Prefrontal Cortex

The most evolved part of the brain; it has already been introduced for its role in executive functioning. The Prefrontal Cortex is central to life's day to day organizing and functioning.

Location:

The front tip of the brain, underneath the forehead.

Prefrontal Cortex Functions:

- Attention span & Concentration
- Planning & Organization
- Communication
- Conscious thought
- Critical thinking
- Judgment

- Impulse control
- Recognition and translation of feelings, such as love, hate or passion
- Feeling and expression of emotions, such as happiness, sadness, joy, and love

Decreased activity in prefrontal cortex:

- Cited in people who are having cognitive difficulty
- Schizophrenia or major depression
- Problems mediating concentration
- Inadequate impulse control
- Impaired critical thinking

The Basal Ganglia

Individuals with anxiety and panic disorders exhibit increased levels of basal ganglia activity.

Location:

It is the area of the brain that surrounds the limbic system. It contains some of the largest structures in the brain.

Basal Ganglia Functions:

- Processing center
- Controls functions critical to human behavior
- Stores patterns of learned behavior
- Stores programming from the past
- Sets the body's idle (stimulation and anxiety level)
- Integrates feelings and movement. (jumping for joy, trembling with nervousness, frozen with fright)

The Cingulate System

The Cingulate system allows you to shift attention from one thing to another.

Location:

The area of the brain at the top, from the middle of the frontal lobes, in and around the brain

Cingulate Functions:

- Feelings of safety and security
- Cognitive flexibility (helps you go with the flow)
- Facilitates shifting of attention
- Helps mind move from idea to idea
- Allows the individual to see options

Increased Cingulate activity:

- Cited as a finding in OCD (Obsessive-Compulsive Disorder, where people become "stuck" on certain thoughts or behaviors)
- Rumination ("stuck" on real or imagined injustices and think about them over and over.)
- Aggressive behavior

The Limbic System

The Limbic system is the part of the brain that sets a person's emotional tone and stores highly charged positive and negative emotional memories.

The Limbic system is where depression and ADD intersect, as well as the seat of the ADD core systems are moodiness, sadness, decreased interest in life and low energy. I included information on the Limbic System because of the frequent occurrence of depression with ADD.

Location:

The limbic system is localized in the sub-cortical area of the center of the brain. It is the size of a walnut.

Limbic System Functions:

- Sets the emotional tone of the mind
- Stores highly changed emotional memories

- Alters mood and emotions
- Modulates motivation
- Affects bonding and social connectedness
- Controls sleep and appetite cycles
- Processes directly the sense of smell
- Modulates the libido

Abnormalities of the Limbic System

- Aggressiveness
- Agitation
- Mood swings

The Temporal Lobes

Temporal lobes are involved with memory, learning, and language. They store memories and images which produce our sense of personal identity and our sense of connectedness to those around us.

Location:

On either side of the brain behind the temples

Temporal Lobe Functions:

When the temporal lobes function normally we have good sense of who we are, our life situations, and the nature of things around us.

Either side of temporal lobe

- Stores memories and images
- Stores our expressions
- Helps us define our sense of ourselves

Dominate Side (usually the left)

- Understanding and processing language
- Short-term memory

- Long-term memory
- Auditory learning
- Retrieval of words
- Complex memories
- Visual and auditory images

Non-Dominant side (usually the right)

- Rhythm
- Music
- Visual learning

Abnormalities in the right temporal lobe:

- Anxiety
- Depression
- Social withdrawal

Abnormalities in the left temporal lobe:

- Irritability
- Aggressiveness and violence (toward others and self)

Neurology and Parts of the Brain Summary

Very Important

The Prefrontal Cortex	The most evolved part of the brain—regulates Executive Functioning (filtering, focusing, deciding, prioritizing, planning, etc.)
The Basal Ganglia	Stores patterns of behavior
The Cingulate System	Supports shifting of attention
The Limbic System	Sets emotional tone
The Temporal Lobes	Stores memories and experiences

3

Getting Diagnosed

It is necessary to get a diagnosis if you think that your teen may have AD/HD. When in doubt refer and request that they get diagnosed. One of the reasons it is so important is to rule out something that isn't AD/HD. They may have another disorder that has similar characteristics as AD/HD. A diagnosis is necessary in order to get medications.

Teens with undiagnosed AD/HD often have a gut feeling that they are different from other kids, but don't know why. These teenagers have been consistently chided that they are lazy and not working up to their ability.

Tired of trying unsuccessfully to please their parents and teachers, they may end up dropping out of school or getting into trouble because of all the anger they have internalized. For some teens, by the time they are diagnosed with ADD, they are ready to give up on themselves, their families and school.

Helping Your Child

Parents often ask, *"What should I do if I suspect my teen has AD/HD? What is my role in helping him?"*

First and foremost, it is extremely important to get a proper diagnosis from a physiatrist, or a neurologist who treats AD/HD.

Try to educate yourself about ADD before you decide whom to use. Interview two or three doctors. Be sure to pick a doctor whom you trust and who has knowledge and experience dealing with all aspects of ADD, ADHD, LD and co-existing disorders.

In the meantime, don't forget to praise and encourage your teen. Look for his good qualities and focus on them. This will help to build up his self-esteem. The most important things a parent can do for a teenager is to listen to him with belief and offer unconditional love, respect and patience. Treat the ADD teen in a firm, structured and respectful way, and he will respond in kind.

The next step is to set up a treatment plan. The treatment plan will be more effective if it involves interaction with all of the individuals seeking to help the AD/HD teenager. The teen, parents, doctors, teachers, and coach should be available to interact with each other if necessary.

Being diagnosed and treated for AD/HD can be a turning point in a teen's life. but it usually takes some time for a teenager to accept the fact that he is different. Immediately following diagnosis, many teens worry about the reaction of their peers. Some teens will swear their families to secrecy about their diagnosis and the medications they are taking.

Teens can also have a negative, angry reaction to finding out that there is something permanently wrong with them. Teens may go through a period of grief and mourning when self-pity can be expected. Recognizing and dealing with a teen's feelings relating to being diagnosed with AD/HD is a necessary step toward making positive decisions for his future.

Family support is critical during this period of adjustment. It is important for a teen to know that there is help and that someone understands what he is going through.

The adults in an ADD teen's life must show confidence in him, enabling the teen to have confidence in himself. This may be difficult, as this period is often stressful for parents too. Teens are sometimes hostile towards their parents, teachers, friends and themselves. Therapy can be helpful in dealing with this anger.

Knowing that there is help from a coach may make a teen less resentful. They are so tired of saying, "You don't understand." When they meet a coach and other individuals with ADD who do understand, it can be a real eye-opener. This experience can have a positive impact on the teen's "self-talk." The following is a scenario is typical of ADD diagnosis and how working with an ADD coach can help.

Paul

Earlier in the school year Paul's tenth grade science teacher called Paul's parents to express her concerns about Paul's performance at school.

Even though Paul isn't a troublemaker, he does stand out in class. He daydreams and stares out the window. He never volunteers and appears not to care. The teacher was concerned that Paul appears to be underachieving and is not as socially mature as his peers.

> Paul has few friends, which makes him a target for name-calling. "Stupid" and "bad" are just a few of the words used by other kids.
>
> Paul is a bright boy, but he isn't working up to his ability. He forgets to write down homework assignments and to bring his books to school. He is almost always late finishing tasks or handing in work.
>
> Paul's teacher suggested that his parents have him evaluated by a doctor. Paul's doctor suggested consulting a neurologist and a psychiatrist as well. After several consultations, Paul is diagnosed with inattentive ADD. When Paul and his mother anxiously ask the doctor to explain ADD and what can be done about it, the doctor suggests that an ADD coach could help explain Paul's diagnosis and help Paul improve his functioning.
>
> Several months later, when Paul is on the right medication and working with a coach, his teacher calls to say she is beginning to see a significant difference in Paul's functioning.

An AD/HD coach can be a positive roll model for the diagnosed teenager. My teenaged clients welcome my help and guidance because, as an ADD adult, I understand them and identify with what they are thinking and experiencing.

They see that I am continually working on self-improvement and that I keep up with the latest research. Because I am a wife, mother, educator, Master Certified Coach, author and artist, they are inspired by my example and see that someone with AD/HD can lead a fulfilling, balanced life. Role modeling is particularly important because how a teen thinks about himself plays an important role in his self-esteem.

Most teenagers with ADD are frequently told that they are lazy and not working up to their ability. They are accused of underachieving in and out of school. They are usually reminded of what they can't do instead of what they can do.

If the adults in a teen's life don't have confidence in him, how can the teen have confidence in himself and develop a positive self-image?

Teens with undiagnosed ADD try numerous times to please their parents and teachers. How frustrating it is for them to spend so much time on their schoolwork and only get by. It is especially difficult when a teen has a friend who is smart, popular and successful. These are the teens that may drop out of school or end up getting in trouble because of all the anger they have internalized.

By the time some teens are diagnosed with AD/HD, they are ready to give up on themselves, their families and school.

Reactions to Diagnosis

Although many teens are relieved to have an explanation for their difficulties, teens can also have a negative, angry reaction to finding out that there is something permanently different about them. They may go through grief and mourning and have a difficult time for quite a while. Teens also worry about having to take necessary medicine, especially in front of their peers. This is a normal process. Time and support help heal the heart.

A newly diagnosed teen needs a lot of psychological support quickly. AD/HD children need to be reassured that they are fine and will feel better about themselves once they get some help with their challenges and goals.

Parents want to be helpful, but they are still coping with their own grief over their teen's diagnosis. Eventually parents will read books and will become more informed about their child's diagnosis, but they rarely have enough information to support their teen from the start.

ADD Coaches can be invaluable during the period immediately following diagnosis, to the parents as well as the teen. I help my clients build on their personal foundation as early as possible, and am willing to explain ADD challenges and interventions to the teen's parents and teachers.

I come to my clients' coaching sessions with my "bag of tools": I validate, endorse, make requests, strategize, praise and encourage.

My teens know that I will encourage them to risk making a mistake. I will listen, validate what they said and ask specific questions about what they did. I ask questions to encourage the teen to think and figure out the answer without my telling them. I speak up occasionally if a client gets off track.

As I remind the parents of my clients, if you are a parent who wants to raise a successful AD/HD child, remember that praise, praise, and more praise are important to your teen. Look for the good qualities in your teenager and focus on them. Your reaction plays an important role in their self-talk and self-esteem. Praise, encouragement, and patience with responsibilities are important tools for parents.

The most important thing a parent can do for teenagers is to listen to them with belief. Listen without passing judgment. Practice unconditional love and respect. ADD teens need to know that their stories, comments, questions and concerns are important to their parents. The more you listen to teens the sooner they will open up to you and a healthy parent/child relationship will develop.

Teens are often told what to do and what they can't do—usually without an explanation. They are told to pay attention, do class work quietly, don't speak unless asking or answering a question. As a result, teens are sometimes hostile toward the parents, teachers and themselves. It might be necessary to address the anger by going into therapy. In therapy, the teen will be work on issues that have affected the teen's life for a long time.

Coaching can be successful as soon as the teen is ready to take the necessary steps to begin self-growth, to work on personal goals and address challenges. Coaching can begin even if the teen is also getting therapy. Generally a partnership between coach and client develops and a client is able to experience much success from the coaching.

Summary

It is necessary for the teen to get properly diagnosed by a physician who is familiar with ADD. It is crucial to the teenager who is diagnose with ADD to be treated as normal as possible and be respected for his differences and individuality. Praise will go much further then criticism.

4

ADD Coaching

What is ADD Coaching?

ADD coaching is a unique and powerful means of helping ADDers to over-come their ADD challenges and reach their goals. Coaching is a partnership with the client which can improve the teens' self-esteem and performance. Coaching assists in the achievement of independence and personal growth. A coach helps to identify a client's goals and facilitate strategies for achieving these goals. The client, in turn, gives the coach ideas about the type of guidance and help he needs. A coach is a guide as well as a personal cheerleader. The coach and teen eventually develop an effective professional relationship.

The primary mode of communication by the coach is asking pertinent questions to get the teenager to think and respond. By asking instead of telling, the notion that the student knows best is reinforced. It also encourages reflection and models the use of thinking to investigate, evaluate, prioritize, plan, and take action. Using this method, the teen often discovers his or her challenges and goals.

A coach listens for language blocks, values and needs, and then evaluates the best way to encourage the teen to take action. Together, the coach and client problem-solve. The coach helps the client to identify and acquire the needed resources for success, and assists in removing material or physical blocks to further progress. By modeling potent questions the coach is actually helping the teen to become her or his own coach.

Through coaching, the teen learns new skills and tools for personal growth, for living a balanced life, and for building a future career. The coach helps the teen to discover his gifts and talents, and by praising and encouraging him, increases his self-esteem tremendously.

A well-informed ADD coach can also take a role in helping clients put together their "team." The professionals on the team can include doctors, psychopharmacologies, social workers, therapists, psychiatrists, neurologists and coaches.

Coaching works best when the teen is motivated and really wants help. When the teen is ready to take the necessary steps to begin self-growth, he can begin to focus on overcoming his challenges successfully and accomplishing his goals.

When parents force coaching on an unwilling teen, it is rarely successful. It is best for parents to take a back seat and let the coach take charge. Eventually, as the coaching progresses successfully, the teen assumes much of the responsibility. A feeling of tension and guilt on the parents' part are often abated over time as progress is made, and the relationship between parent and child improves through clearer communication.

In order to better appreciate the benefits of coaching, it is crucial to understand the differences between coaching and therapy. Many people incorrectly assume that if their child is in therapy, he doesn't need coaching.

The following, condensed from the A.C.T. Coaching Manual with permission, are some of the differences between coaching and therapy:

- Coaching is "who" based and focuses on actions towards value-based goals.

- Therapy is "why" based and focuses on feelings. Therapy follows a medical model and is usually covered under health insurance.

- A coach's methods of helping a client include clarification, encouragement, information and praise.

- A therapist's main tools are confrontation and interpretation.

- In therapy, the patient isn't allowed to know personal details of a therapist's life. There are strong boundaries in therapy involving legal and ethical limits and guidelines.

- While ADD coaches are also professionals and are careful to maintain appropriate boundaries, a coach may ethically share relevant personal information with a client.

- If the coaches also have ADD, it is not unusual for them disclose some of their own ADD challenges, especially if they relate closely to those of the client, to demonstrate that ADD challenges can be overcome successfully.

The coach's mode of questioning

Teens bring their personal and academic agenda to their coaching sessions. The coach asks the teenager questions, empowering her to focus on ways of developing external stimuli. The teen begins to trust the coach and finds motivation returns, providing the impetus for action that will result in evidence of success.

Helping teens search for their gifts is crucial for their self-esteem. Most ADD teens are original, creative, fascinating, inventive, talented, daring, funny, sensitive and compassionate. It is generally easier for a coach to begin this process of searching for gifts than the teen's parents, who have many memories of the teen's struggles prior to diagnosis.

The best teachers for ADD children have clear rules and expectations and also use their heads and hearts to tell them when and how to modify the rules. Once parents realize that it is perfectly normal for teens to have an attitude and, under the best circumstances, teens and parents personalities clash or don't mesh well together, the parents are relieved and no longer feel guilty. At that point their relationship with their teen improves.

A coach can act as a mediator between parents and teens, having a positive effect in the relationship with the whole family. Toms' story on the next few pages is an example of this dynamic.

The Coaching Prep Form

The Coaching Prep Form gives both client and coach a record of the client's progress and focuses the client before the session. It consists of some basic questions that the client answers every week before his coaching session. Each client emails or faxes the completed form to his coach and prints a copy to keep in front of him or her during the session. This form A session can get off track whenever something else important to the teen comes up. I get the teen back on track if what is being talked about strays away from coaching. During our current session the teen determines what she will accomplish by our next session and she will write it on the form as the session concludes as a reminder.

Coaching Prep Form Questions

A Standard Coaching Prep Form will include some version of the following questions:

- **What did you accomplish since our last session?**
- **What didn't you accomplish that you wanted to?**
- **What challenges are you facing now?**
- **What opportunities do you have?**
- **How do you want to focus this coaching session?**
- **What will you do by next week?**

Many teens do not like to do the prep form before each session initially, but the small amount of homework that the teen does before the session allows the teen to stay on track for the session and more than doubles its effectiveness.

Most teens work well with a coach if they are motivated. When teens want help they will work efficiently with a coach. I might ask a teen who is forced into coaching and isn't responsive after several sessions to consider stopping. Coaching is client oriented and a teen will only benefit if he takes action, does what he said he will do, and takes responsibility for himself. That rarely happens if the teen is participating in coaching only because his parents insist.

ADHD, along with typical teen hormonal changes, can cause barriers between teens and parents. A coach can act as a mediator on the whole family.

I make a request to teen's parents to please take a back seat and let me work with the teen alone. Many parents are reluctantly relieved to give me the responsibility at the beginning. Once the teen understands the concept of coaching, however, I place the responsibility where it belongs—with the teenager.

As coaching progresses and with the consent of your client, it is important for the coach to include the parents in the decisions that are being made, and to explain to the parents that is happening and what is being accomplished.

The coach must make sure the teen is comfortable with this communication so that he will not feel like his parents and coach are talking about him behind his back. The teen's rights to confidentiality must being respected in the same manner that those of an adult client. Trust between client and coach is essential, whatever the age of the client.

Toms' Story

I am coaching a seventeen year old male named Tom, who has ADHD.

His mother contacted me a year ago, when she was at her wits' end. She told me that she was tired of fighting with him about doing his homework, studying and doing simple chores. Getting him to bed at a reasonable hour and waking him in the morning were ordeals for her.

Tom was extremely hyperactive from the time he was a small boy. As a six-year-old, he would climb out of the window and run across the roof. As he got older, he would climb trees and jump down from dangerous heights, knowing that it might hurt him.

As a teen, he would run from room to room around the house. When Tom sat down at the dinner table he would sing loudly, drum on the table, interrupt people as they ate, and take a long time to eat because he could not focus on his food.

Tom had problems at school as well. He was impulsive, disorganized, couldn't concentrate, and frequently paid no attention to his teachers. He had just started a new school after having been asked to leave his last school. This had been a pattern for the last five years.

Even though he was hyperactive, he was introverted and had low self-esteem. At the time his mother contacted me, she informed me that he was seeing a psychiatrist and taking medication. He had been diagnosed several years ago yet continued to have problems with school, time management, and social skills.

When I met Tom, he appeared to be shy, angry and withdrawn. Once we spoke privately, Tom confessed that he knew that he needed whatever help he could get. I praised Tom for the courage it took to admit that to me.

He spoke and I listened without interrupting him. Out came fears, concerns and questions that he was afraid to ask his parents. He expressed his desire to succeed and began to come to me for weekly coaching sessions.

In our sessions together, the first thing we did was to prioritize what Tom wanted to focus on for the week. One week he might focus on that day's homework and another week on studying for an exam.

I asked Tom the questions and he figured out the answers. Together we set long and short-term goals, focusing on overcoming challenges that might make it difficult to achieve these goals. I was also able to monitor Tom's medication and make some suggestions to his doctor. After minor modifications were made, his medications were working better than ever.

Eight months after our coaching began; Tom is one of my best clients. He studies and does homework on a daily basis without having to be reminded. Not only have his grades gone from D's to A's and B's, but his behavior in school has improved as well.

Tom is thriving and becoming a responsible, reliable, likable teenager. He has a thirst for learning that he never expressed before.

Over the summer he worked two jobs and, without being asked, he took pride in keeping his family's lawn ship-shape. He is practicing driving and saving his money for a car and car insurance.

It has been very rewarding for me to watch him grow and accomplish, and his family is thrilled with his progress.

Tom wanted to write the following endorsement of the coaching process and I am pleased to have his permission to share his experience of our coaching relationship in his own words.

"Hi! My name is Tom and I am seventeen years old. Before I started working with Mrs. Walker, my ADHD coach, I had no idea how to get and keep myself organized. I could not make myself a schedule and stick to it or complete tasks that I started.

I was the king of procrastination. My report cards always said that I didn't complete my homework. Even though I had been on Ritalin since I was in fifth grade, there were always obstacles in the way of my being productive. Later I learned that the Ritalin was helping a little bit, but it still wasn't the best medication for me. Eventually I made the switch to Adderall, which is working great!

When I started coaching, I was skeptical. After a few months of coaching, I began noticing a dramatic change in my productivity. I found myself more organized in school as well as at home.

A great reason to use a coach is that people, especially people with AD/HD, like to take real action when there is a problem. Based on my own personal experience, I feel that along with the right dose of medicine, getting an AD/HD coach is the best way to tackle AD/HD. A coach teaches you the skills that you will actually use in order to take action against the problems associated with AD/HD.

Mrs. Walker taught me how to prioritize the things I have to do, how to make a schedule, stick to a routine, and develop social skills. She also gave me the tools to help me keep myself from procrastinating and wasting time. Even though I still think I have a long way to go, coaching has dramatically changed my life."

Systems Development Coaching

There are currently many specialties of coaches. A Systems Development Coach teaches clients time management, organizational and study skills, prioritizing and planning, and guides clients in developing systems for achieving their goals, always breaking things down into manageable steps.

- A coach also promotes productive thinking and problem solving, helping clients to avoid self-pity, procrastination and self-punishment.

- A coach provides guidance and encouragement, fosters self-awareness and self-esteem.

- A coach provides structure, assists in prioritizing, establishing routines and good habits.

- A knowledgeable ADD coach helps monitor effectiveness and side-effects of medication.

This is my specialty, and I enjoy it immensely.

The following client story will show you how Systems Development Coaching worked with a client named Irene.

Irene

Irene is a sixteen-year-old with a combination of ADD and inattentive ADHD. We originally concentrated on school-related challenges, but it quickly became obvious that she needed help in other areas as well.

Irene wanted to clean and organize her room which, when I first arrived, looked like it had been hit by a hurricane. For three weeks, during her regular coaching session, we spent two hours working on this difficult task.

Step by step, we cleaned, sorted and organized. Most importantly, we took notes on what we were doing so that Irene would eventually be able to do this on her own. Her homework was to do the same thing in the two drawers in her desk by our next session.

The final step was for me to watch her straighten out her room on her own, with her notes at hand. Breaking down the chores and taking notes enabled her to finish the project feeling proud and accomplished instead of frustrated, angry and overwhelmed by the mess.

The next item that Irene wanted to work on was time management. She confessed that she was consistently late for school, classes, papers, homework and appointments.

I asked Irene if she had a school or day planner. She replied that she never used it. She did write things down on sticky notes but kept losing them. I taught her how to use a planner and we worked on modifying it to her needs.

We spent one mouth on problems and solutions regarding time management. Irene answered my questions and together we developed systems for each of her challenges.

Irene would go on tackling one challenge at a time until I was no longer needed.

ADD Summary

ADD coaching is a powerful way of guiding teens to understand their disorder as long as the teens themselves want help to improve their lives. There may be a need first to have an understanding of ADD before one may want to consider hiring a coach. ADD is a complex and challenging disorder.

People having a considerable amount of contact with a teen that has been recently diagnosed, or one who has some of the characteristics of ADD and has yet to be diagnosed, need to have some foundation about ADD to be helpful. An ADD Coach can help here as well.

5

Coaching Skills

The Basic Coaching Techniques

Among other things, coach training is designed to transfer skills that successful coaches use with their clients. Student coaches are taught how to help people overcome their challenges and achieve their goals. Coaches-in-training attend coaching workshops where they role-play numerous techniques. Some of the most important ADD Coaching Skills are listed below.

Listening is one of the Core Coaching skills, and "listening from belief" is the most important thing a coach can do.

Coaches listen intently; feel compassion and (most of the time) believes that their clients are representing their situation accurately, even when the evidence might seem to suggest something else.

If a teenager is willing to get help and acknowledges that he needs a coach, generally he does not lie. He is told from the beginning of the coach/client relationship that what he says is confidential. A good coach listens to the client's truthful account of his or her reality; gauges emotion and notes strengths and challenges.

Languaging is another Core Coaching skill, a particular way of endorsing and validating what the teen is saying. How a coach "languages" determines how the teen understands what is being said to him.

With **identifying**, one of the ADD Coach Lang aging Skills, a coach shares ADD information and helps the teen recognize the ADD specific issues as coaching progresses.

It is common for an ADD Coach to **advise** clients and to make **requests** of them. Coaches relate to their clients by communicating through spoken language, **clarifying** what the teen heard and understood, as well as through body language.

When communicating effectively, a good ADD coach looks for opportunities to "cheerlead" or **endorse**.

Advising is accomplished through messaging in several types and making requests from the teen.

Challenging is prompting, directing, and standing for your client's highest abilities.

Distinguishing is being able to ascertain what the client is really saying, where the client is coming from, and the ability to **reframe** ways of approaching life by using a slightly different term.

Relating includes connecting with the teen, getting what is said, dancing conversationally, and loving your clients.

Strategizing is the approach used to prioritize the coaching; the importance, where to begin, and what can they handle.

Strategies are developed to help the teen achieve his goals. Clients learn where to begin a task and what they have to do to handle it successfully.

Modeling is setting a good example by the way you function for your teen client. It is very common for a coach to model what she is saying by setting an example. She may use her life experiences to help the teen understand.

Basic Language Skills

Here are some of the techniques learned by ADD coaches that are useful to anyone dealing with an ADD teen.

Endorsing:	Validating and "cheerleading" to make the teen feel valuable, increasing self-esteem. A coach listens for reasons to endorse. **Example:** *"I read your essay and it was wonderful!"*
Responding:	Making sure the teen feels heard, including the coaches reaction to what was said. **Examples:** He complains he can never find his notebook. *"You keep misplacing your notebook."* She discusses a problem with a teacher. *"It sounds like the teacher doesn't really understand your point of view, is that how it seems to you?"*

Mirroring

A way of responding that can be used by client or coach. The coach can repeat a version of what the teen said to her or have the teen repeat back what the coach just said.

Examples:

After a description of a particularly difficult exam, the coach responds with mirroring, *"So even though it was a really tough exam that might have thrown you, you identified your challenges and worked around them where necessary."*

The coach ends an explanation of homework systems with, *"Now, let's go over your notes to make sure you are clear. How would you describe what I just said?"*

Clarifying:

Helping a client get clear on what they are experiencing, or giving them the opportunity to tell the truth without shame.

Example: "Tom, did you leave your homework in your locker or forget to do it?"

Requesting:

Stating desires simply and directly.

Example: *"Sara, please collect the tests and put them on my desk."*

Relating:

Connecting with what the teen is saying.

Example: *"I can imagine how you feel when your dad starts yelling at you. I shut down when people yell at me."*

Strategizing:

Suggest an actual approach to take to figure things out.

Example: *"Cross off each thing on your list as you do it."*

This skill also refers to the coach's approach to the client's coaching.

Example: *"She will need to understand her ADD challenges before I can begin to work with her study skills, and her meds need to be adjusted before we can do either of those…"*. and so on.

Advising:

Messaging; pointing out observations as a way of instructing a teen.

Example: *"You keep losing your keys. Put your keys in one place when you get home, such as a small basket."*

Mapping:

Distinguishing small steps toward goals.

Example: *"Doing your homework at the same time each day will help you develop the homework habit Placing it in your book bag by the door as soon as it is done will help you hand it in on time. How will you remember to turn it in?"*

Modality—The way people learn

Whether I coach high school, college students or adults I find out the modalities they use for learning, looking for the various ways they process information. I especially encourage teens to understand how they learn and process. The ways I ask my questions help my teenagers figure out their answers.

It is very difficult to stay focused in a language that is not your own. Teens will be able to hear you better if you speak to them in their native tongue. That is where modality comes into play.

Being able to tape lectures may be helpful. Inference is a common learning disability which may present a challenge to many students. It is difficult for some ADD teens to read between the lines. By incorporating different modalities in teaching, a larger number of teens will find a way to learn.

I believe that as a coach it is my responsibility to help and partner with my clients, young and old. How individuals process information and how they learn are necessary to know in order for my clients to want to achieve their full potential and lead a successful life.

The following material is from Madelyn Griffith–Haynie's A.C.T. Program Manual (©1994), elements explaining her theories about linking and learning; it is reproduced with permission.

The Dominant Modality is the modality a teen naturally uses when learning takes place most reliably.

The Preferred Modality is the modality a teen uses *habitually*. It may or may not be their dominant modality. It is often a product of conditioning and training (similar to left-handers trained by teachers to use their right hand.)

Types of Modality—ways people learn

Visual: What the teen **sees**
Example: One visual client doesn't like to see clutter on his desk. Another inadvertently creates clutter because "out of sight out of mind."

Audio: What the teen **hears**
Example: Some teens can be coached on the phone and understand clearly, others may prefer to be coached in person but will tend to look away while they listen to better concentrate on what they are hearing instead of what they are seeing.

Verbal:	What the teen **says** **Example:** Tom is much more likely to remember a list if he repeats the items aloud, or to recall the point of the story if asked to summarize to the listener.
Tactile:	What a teen experiences through the sense of touch. **Example:** Kim brings in pieces of fur and a rock to science class and concentrates better when she has something to "fidget" with.
Kinesthetic:	Related to body positioning and inner feelings of positional comfort and memory. It's the most <u>reliable</u> modality for most people, but not always their dominant. **Example:** A teen tells you how she felt when she was asked to the prom. You can watch her body position changing as she remembers.
Cerebral:	Cognitive thinking, with the details linked to the big picture. **Example:** A client learns better by reviewing notes taken in class or by having an outline of the points as he listens to the lecture to refer too.

How Coaches Determine a Client's Modalities

Most clients are a mix of modalities (cerebral/kinesthetic/visual etc.). They don't know how they process best. Many teens have been socialized away from their dominant modality.

For example:

- A verbal dominant raised by a cognitive dominant may have been taught that interrupting is rude so is not in touch with his need to process aloud to anchor the learning, so he thinks he can't learn.

- A cognitive dominant raised by a verbal dominant may have been urged to attempt to think aloud, even though her thoughts weren't well-formed enough to verbalize, leading her to believe she was slow or dense.

- A visual dominant may have been taught to read and spell through phonics, never really seeing how that was supposed to work—so it didn't.

- An audile dominant may have been taught to read using pattern recognition and now wonders why she can't read very well and learns best with books on tape.

The "Sherlock Holmes" method:

The client states a problem. The coach's job is to listen for clues about the way to language questions about the problem on the way to figuring out the steps that will lead the client on a journey of self-discovery. *"Let's talk about how you did it the last time,"* would be a way of talking to a verbal processor.

Listen to what your ADD teen tells you: their subconscious knows their dominant modality and their language will reflect it.

Coaches often identify client modalities by listening for what is known as a client's "Aha!" statement, what they say when the suddenly understand a concept that formerly escaped them:

- *"I see!"*
- *"I hear you,"* or *"That sounds right."*
- *"Let me see if I have that right"* (and then they rephrase it) or *"In other words..."*
- *"Yeah, that feels right,"* or *"I was having grasping that, but now I do."*
- *"Oh, I get it,"* or *"That fits."*
- *"NOW I understand."*

It is very important to learn which modalities work best for each client and for ourselves. It is a real gift to transfer the skill of identifying the way we take in information and how we process it: how we integrate information, link it for retrieval and use it as we approach the tasks of our lives.

Coaching Skills Summary

Coaches come to the coaching arena with a variety of coaching tools.

I cannot emphasize enough how important it is to figure out what learning modalities work best for an individual that you are teaching or communicating with, at home, school or on the job.

It is a great idea to have the teen repeat back to you, not only to see if she understood, but also to hear the language of modality with which she communicates that understanding.

6

Coaching Solutions for ADD Challenges

People with ADD face many challenges on a daily basis. Things that come naturally to most people are often difficult for people with this challenging disorder. There are various steps which, when taken, can have a positive effect on people with ADD. What are some of these common challenges?

Attending

Teens with untreated ADD may have a difficult time paying attention and concentrating on what they are supposed to be learning. They may have difficulty with teachers' lectures, class work, tests and homework. Difficulty sustaining attention will be most apparent during "boring" or unexciting experiences, including reading and schoolwork. They may also have reading and retention difficulties. They also may be easily overwhelmed by tasks of daily living.

Immediate intervention is necessary. This could include medication, therapy, coaching and education. Consistent positive reinforcement is also necessary to help overcome attention difficulties.

Impulsivity and Hyperactivity

The related challenges to this are hyperactivity, low stress tolerance, impulsivity and mood swings. Stress intolerance may result in confusion; difficulty making decisions, anger and depression. Teens may also have difficulty delaying gratification and stimulation seeking. The same treatment that is recommended for attending problems is appropriate for this and most other AD/HD challenges.

Memory Problems

It is very common for teens with AD/HD to have difficulty with their short-term memory, even though they may be very intelligent. Sometimes, they forget names, where they put things, dates, birthdays and agreements. They may even forget to meet people, with whom they had appointments, including their friends.

Coaching, medication, and counseling can be helpful. A coach can give little cues that will help them remember. Better yet, the coach will ask the client to think of his own cues and ideas on how he can remember. Making him aware that this difficulty is due to AD/HD (and not stupidity) is a relief to most clients.

Low Self Esteem

Below are several basic ways to establish and enhance self-esteem.

- Incorporate open discussion and feedback in your communications

- Utilize peer groupings and activities.

- Respect individual differences and learning styles.

- Utilize problem-solving strategies and higher order thinking skills.

- Provide well-defined and positive expectations.

- Provide flexible assignments.

- Develop the client's sense of responsibility.

- Provide "success experiences."

- Omitting self talk such as…*"I can't", "I shouldn't", "I have to", "I always", "I never", "I'll finish later"* along with *"There's plenty of time."*

Disorganization

Teens with AD/HD have trouble with scheduling and staying organized. It is helpful to make a checklist for routines in the morning, after school, and evening. These checklists may be very detailed. For example, the morning schedule may include brushing teeth, showering, eating breakfast, making the bed, and taking book bag and/or lunch. Teens may also want to work with a coach to create an afternoon and evening schedule. The coach asks the questions and the teen figures out the schedule. There is always room for modification.

Regular times may be scheduled for doing homework and studying. Schedule homework and study times into a daily planner. During these times, regular 15 to 30 minute breaks could be scheduled in order to allow the teen to stay focused.

If a teen's handwriting is messy, he can use an erasable pen, or do his work on a computer. If possible, have a peer in every class make sure the teen client writes homework assignments and takes notes, or agrees to do this for him if the client can't.

It can be helpful to color code notebooks or loose leafs in order to find them in a hurry. I encourage my clients to put their filled book bag next to the door they exit in the morning, the night before. I also remind them to pick out their clothes for the next day before going to bed.

Perfectionism

Perfectionism and black and white thinking are common problems among people with AD/HD. In order to counteract this, it is important for the teen to establish priorities, set realistic expectations, and realize that no one expects him to be perfect all of the time.

I discourage teens from getting angry at themselves simply because they make a mistake. I remind them that mistakes can be a valuable learning experience. Together we develop a system to make the teen less stressed in what he/she is trying to accomplish. It is more important to complete the job then ruminate over getting it perfect.

Poor Listening Skills

If a teen is not listening to you, it can sometimes be helpful to whisper to him, forcing him to listen more closely. To help concentrate; sometimes it is helpful for the teen to be given something to fidget with. You can use a squeeze ball, silly putty, or just let the teen doodle while he is listening. Having the teen repeat instructions you have given him can help him to remember. A coach will ask questions to see if the teen "got it."

Difficulty Processing and Learning

Teenagers learn by various methods, including visual, auditory, kinesthetic, verbal, cerebral and tactile. Usually, people learn by a combination of these modalities.

Knowing the different modalities by which a person learns and processes information is extremely important to the student as well as the teacher or coach. In order to effectively help a client achieve his potential, the coach must determine how the client processes information and learns.

Students with AD/HD frequently have trouble keeping up with the speed of the teacher and the rest of the class. These teens may have problems processing the intake of information due to their wandering minds. An AD/HD brain may drift to another place in order to avoid the confusion and frustration of not understanding. A knowledgeable teacher will use multi-sensory instruction, combining a variety of teaching techniques in order to reach all the students, including those with ADD. By using different modalities in teaching, a larger number of teens will be able to learn.

Inference Problems

People with AD/HD have a difficult time with inference. Inference stands for something that is derived of a conclusion by reasoning of something inferred or assumed. Someone or a passage from a book may be referring by description to something without actually saying what it is. It is up to you to know what is meant. The expression reading between the lines refers to **inference. It is therefore crucial to be precise and exact** about what you want the teen to do.

For example, instead of saying *"Study the study guide I gave you for the test,"* say *"Study the study guide I gave you; most of it will be on the test. Focus on the questions and answers you did for homework."* With the help of a coach, the teen can become more familiar with inference and eventually understand it better.

Challenges with Time Management

Time management is a major challenge for many people, not just those with AD/HD. It is common for ADD teens to be late to school, classes and appointments. This is sometimes an indirect consequence of the fact that they have sleep disorders. Some ADD teens may lie in bed for hours before falling asleep. Others take prescribed medication to be administered at bedtime, which may cause extreme drowsiness which still affects them when it is time to wake up. It is also easy for a teen to loose track of time, under-or over-estimating how long something is going to take.

To help with time management, a coach encourages teens to:

- Use a daily planner (see below) or Palm Pilot.
- Prioritize daily.
- Create "to do," "to get," "to call," "to go" lists each night
- Lay out clothes, shoes and book bag each night.
- Take a shower in the evening.
- Prepare lunch in the evening.

Use of a daily planner

Most ADD teens do not know how to correctly use a daily planner or Palm Pilot. Unless they have been taught step by step how to use these tools, they usually shy away from them. Some planners I recommend are Day Timer, Franklin Covey, and Day Runner. I prefer two pages to a day and a monthly planner inserted as well.

I also teach clients to use lined Post-its. On the post-its make lists: **To Do, To Go, To Get, To Buy,** and **To Call**. Put the post-it over the daily notes page. Things can still be written on the daily notes page. They have the advantage of taking just the post it with them if they wish.

A daily planner can be helpful for remembering homework assignments, appointments, school activities, chores, quizzes, exams, projects, break time and just about anything a teen needs to remember. Different types and colors of ink can be used to color code the planner for easy reference.

A coach should encourage teens to get either a daily planner or an electric organizer and teach them exactly how to use it, praising them as they become more adept. Teens can even be told to reward themselves with a treat or extra computer time etc. at the end of the day when they correctly use their planners.

Procrastination

Procrastination is putting off doing something until later. Teens often procrastinate for several reasons. They may not know where to begin, they don't understand the directions, the task or homework may be difficult for them, or they have too many projects going on at the same time. Getting help can help prevent procrastination and decrease anxiety.

The following tips may help with procrastination:

- Plan ahead what you have to do, either weeks or the day before.

- Divide what you have to do into steps or chunks. For example, if you are cleaning and organizing your desk, divide it mentally into three or more sections you can even draw a sketch if you are a visual learner.

- Clear off, put away and clean one section a day for three days.

- Don't put off what you have to do today, especially for school.

- Have a steno pad handy to write down your ideas.

- Use a timer, alarm watch, or alarm clock.

- Start early in the day and tell yourself you are going to be productive. Tell yourself, "If I don't do it, it won't get done."

- Don't fall into the "Do-It-All" trap. Delegate, when necessary.

Social Skills

The majority of the teens whom I coach complain that they don't know how to communicate well with other teenagers. To most teens his comes naturally, but not to ADD teens. It is very common for them to experience their share of social problems.

Due to poor attentiveness, shyness, and distractibility, it is difficult for the teen to focus on what is important in social interaction. AD/HD teens sometimes do appear different and behave in unusual ways. They sometimes become targets for bullies and are routinely harassed in school.

Once a teen is on the right medication with the correct dose, the teen is generally more aware of himself and his surroundings. Slowly their behavior begins to change. As a coach, I am always doing reality checks to determine how well my clients are processing information, and I check on their level of social skills as well.

I usually ask clients if they have friends, and whether or not they make plans together. Once a teen acknowledges the difficulty he has getting and keeping friends, I ask him some questions.

- *Why do you think you don't have friends?*
- *Have you always had a problem with this?*
- *Do you want to do things with other teens?*

- *What do you do over the weekend?*

The answers to these questions usually break the ice and the teen confesses that he social problems. Of course, he also gives excuses like "the other kids are boring, nasty" and so on, but he does let me know he is aware there is a problem.

TOM

Tom, a 17-year-old client with AD/HD, once confided in me that he has only a few friends and that they lived an hour away from him. He told me that most of his classmates were only interested in "partying," which did not interest him…He said he was more intellectual and, although he likes to have fun, he prefers activities other than partying.

After asking a few more questions, Tom admitted that he is shy in front of a group of kids. When they are speaking together, he just stands mutely by, never knowing exactly when he is expected to speak. He eventually told me that the other kids didn't like him, and that they didn't talk to him in school.

I explained to Tom that the group's failure to ask his opinion didn't mean they didn't like him. It was likely that from their point of view, I proposed, they were talking and he was listening. They may have been respecting his choice to remain silent, believing that was how he preferred it.

I asked him if it would be easier for him to start by socializing with one friend at a time, slowly working his way up to larger groups through the friends he felt comfortable with already. He agreed that it probably would be easier to start small and concentrated on his friendship with Ben.

School ended for the year and Tom got a summer job at a day camp. Ben moved nearby for the summer to attend a local camp. Initially, Tom was too busy working to make any new friends at his own camp, but Ben invited him to join him at the camp he attended. Tom went to Bens' camp several evenings and met some of Ben's friends. After a period of time, a few of them began to do things together, and Tom began to feel like he finally understood how to make friends.

Boggle

Today is your turn to get up before your class and give your oral English report. Friday is your Spanish midterm. Your Social Studies term paper is due

Monday. This afternoon you are going to the orthodontist. The remainder of the week you will baby-sit; do your chores, and homework.

Your self-talk is on the negative side, *"How am I going to get through the week?"* Tests, appointments, chores, and studying have you boggling. Having to get up in front of your class to do your oral report will definitely make you boggle. You constantly worry that your mind will go blank when you get nervous.

Boggle. What does that word mean and how does it affect ADD teenagers?

Boggle is a word coined by MGH to describe that state of cognitive shutdown in response to stress. Boggle is frustration, anxiety, fear, and stage-fright all wrapped up in one.

The consequences of boggling are similar to having a panic attack as a result of over-stimulation. Boggle is sweaty palms, a queasy stomach and heartburn all at the same time. Boggle is freezing up and not being able to get the words out of your mouth. Your brain stops functioning. As a result, your behavior may appear strange.

Understanding how boggle affects teens is important in understanding the teen.

Being sympathetic with them is a key part of finding a solution, but the solution to boggle will be temporary unless you develop a system for when it happens. Relief will begin to replace boggle, as soon as the teen takes action.

There is nothing worse to a teen than being embarrassed, especially in front of their peers. Being called on and not being able to respond is frustrating. Even though you may know the answer, you get nervous and you boggle.

It may be necessary to speak with your psychiatrist if you have constant anxiety. Talk to your parents if you feel that nothing else is working and anxiety medication may be necessary. .

Developing systems to address the trouble spots in a teen's life is crucial for a teen with ADD.

ADD teens need initial assistance as they learn to chunk the parts of tasks like schoolwork, daily assignments, studying, and longer reports and projects into manageable steps. Baby steps always come before running.

We may have already discussed when to do work and when to take breaks and the need to write their schedules in their planners rather than relying on memory. It is not unusual for an ADD teen to hear information several times before it sinks in, and most may still need help getting into action initially.

Getting help from a coach in a non-threatening way is a surefire way to reduce the likelihood of boggle. As evidence of success mounts, self-esteem is consistently improving, especially if they are getting guidance and encouragement from your coach.

Sara

Sara just returned home from school. She is tired, hungry, frustrated, and needs some food and down time. Sara's mom reminds her to do her homework, clean her room, take out the garbage and walk the dog. Sara yells at her mom to leave her alone and then stomps out of her room.

What could have been said or done to get cooperation from Sara instead of boggling her? As Sara's coach, I would encourage her to request her mom's permission to get a snack and have one hour of down time before starting homework and chores. As Sara's coach, I would speak to her mom if necessary as long as Sara approves of the homework/short-break system.

I would suggest to Sara to set a timer to go off in one hour. When the alarm rings, Sara is to start her homework without her mom having to tell her to do so. I would ask Sara for her input also. How does she think she should handle it?

By Sara taking the necessary action, the anxiety and boggle will decrease for Both Sara and her mom. They both win; Sara is displaying that she can take responsibility and her mother is showing trust and understanding in Sara.

To reduce anxiety in ADD teens, you can suggest that they:

- work hard and take breaks
- reward yourself for completion, good grades and accomplishments
- put steno pads in the room being occupied to jot down ideas as they arise
- use spell-check on computers
- write schoolwork and homework in something erasable
- doodle if it helps you concentrate
- use a tension ball with permission
- learn self-hypnosis and use it when necessary
- practice any sort of oral presentation in front of a mirror
- focus their eyes on an object during oral exams

More about TOM

Remember Tom, the 17-year-old who was awkward in groups—the one who felt that the other kids didn't like him because they didn't talk to him at school?

The fact that Tom didn't know the appropriate social cues letting him know when it was appropriate to enter into the conversation made him feel awkward and defensive

When Ben introduced Tom to his camp friends, Tom was initially frustrated when his feelings of awkwardness returned. When more than a few of them gathered, Tom told me the feeling was just like having anxiety, fear, and stage fright all wrapped up in one whenever they tried to include him in their conversation. He still didn't know exactly how he was expected to respond.

Since Boggle wasn't far behind his feeling of awkwardness, his first instinct was to avoid interacting with groups to avoid Boggle, even though he wasn't aware of the concept until I explained it after a particular incident he reported to me.

We had to work with the concept of Boggle before Tom was ready to move on. He sincerely wanted to have friends, but he didn't understand how to do that without Boggle.

Once Tom was able to manage his anxiety to the point where he no longer feared Boggle, he was able to enjoy interacting with larger groups.

The "symptoms" of Boggle are similar to those of a panic attack: sweaty palms, a queasy stomach and heartburn. For example, although many teens know the answer to the teacher's question when called on, they sometimes experience performance anxiety so high they can't get words to come out of their mouths. That's another form of Boggle. Needless to say, when an ADD teen boggles his behavior appears strange; which can cause extreme embarrassment.

Understanding and empathy for the teen going through this is an important part of finding the solution. A system must be developed for dealing with Boggle and other trouble spots in an ADD teen's life. The coach needs to assist teens in breaking down tasks, schoolwork, homework, studying, reports and projects into manageable steps. Feeling prepared will allow the teen to feel calmer and increase his self-esteem. Sometimes, medication can help to relieve extreme anxiety. A need for medication can be determined by the teen's parents and psychiatrist.

Anger

Anger is very common in teens and adults with AD/HD. Anger is a feeling of displeasure and hostility resulting from poor self esteem, mistreatment, opposition, frustration, worry, distress or sorrow. Children who have been called troublemakers, stupid, lazy, crazy, daydreamers, hyperactive, disruptive, selfish, underachievers or rebellious risk becoming very angry teenagers. This anger will only get worse if intervention, kindness, understanding, hope, help, empathy and therapy aren't incorporated into their lives. An angry teen with untreated ADD is like a time bomb waiting to explode. At worst, these teens can become juvenile delinquents or adult criminals. Intervention and positive support must happen as early as possible.

We do not want to turn these gifted teens into juvenile delinquents. Another outcome of ignoring their anger is producing very angry AD/HD adults. Can you imagine carrying that anger with you for eight years or more? No wonder our criminal justice system have so many AD/HD criminals in jail. We can't let that continue to happen. Intervention and positive support must be done while kids are still young. Parents, siblings, peers, teachers, psychiatrists, therapists, coaches and educators should all be involved in helping our teens to be respectable adults.

A coach can help teens validate anger and slowly eliminate the obstacles that caused it. Family, friends, educators, psychiatrists, therapists and coaches should all be involved in helping AD/HD teens to become respectable adults.

Rumination

Ruminating is obsessive focusing on negative thoughts, leading to anxiety and frustration. In order to stop this, thoughts must be consciously reprogrammed.

There are several ways of dealing with rumination, including the following:

- Pick a time each day to ruminate for a specific time period, for example 30 minutes at 4 o'clock in the afternoon.
- Give yourself permission to think about something else.
- Write what you are worried about in a steno pad so that you can put it away and forget about it.
- Have a network of people who will listen that you can call.

A Summary of Coaching Tips and Tools for ADD Teens

Many of the ideas mentioned above are useful in various circumstances. Some of the best are in the lists below. Some items and ideas are new, and some were mentioned in this chapter.

Helpful Tools

- Files sorted by color
- Small hourly alarm clock and timer
- Erasable pen
- Organizer or appointment book
- Cell phone or pager
- Phone with headset
- Computer
- Organized and clean workspace
- A coach

Helpful Tips

- Know your strengths and weaknesses.
- Make check lists for routines for the morning, evening, planning, studying, taking breaks, eating, etc. (Be specific about when to get ready for school, brush your teeth, shower, eat breakfast, etc.)
- If permitted, have a friend in every class make sure you write down your homework assignments and take notes.
- Have a daily time to do homework, projects and study.
- Put 15-30 minute breaks into homework time after working steadily for an hour or so.
- Keep samples of dated work in a notebook to chart your progress.
- If your handwriting is messy, use an erasable pen.
- Plan the next day.

- Bullet and prioritize your schedule and your responsibilities.

- Use an organizer appointment book.

- Use separate color pens or highlighters to indicate activities for yourself, your family and for school (or work).

- Use a cell phone or pager away from home so your parents can reach you, for an emergency or for reminders.

- Use caller ID to screen calls and don't give the number to your friends unless they understand your distractibility.

7

Successful Time Management for AD/HD Teens

Time management skills are one of the biggest challenges for ADD teens, usually accomplished successfully only when a number of other areas are considered as well.

Sara

Sara ran out the door without her homework running for the bus. She missed the school bus—again! This time she would miss recess for five days.

She was completely fed up with herself. *"Why I do this? How can I change?"*

Although she was considered a high achiever by most standards, the seemingly simple stuff like being on time and remembering her homework was difficult for her. Some unexpected occurrence always seemed to get in the way. Attaining personal goals and doing well in school were occasionally an issue for Sarah.

Managing all of the activities necessary to get good grades and have a successful school experience was a tricky business for Sarah. She struggled to leave early enough to arrive on time, to remember to put her papers in her book bag the night before, to put the book bag near the door, to track and complete projects, to do all assigned homework nightly, to attend scheduled after school activities, as well as to complete chores at home expected by her parents.

Sarah certainly needed to make some changes: she needed to develop strategies to allow her to be on time. to accomplish her needs and to satisfy her wants.

51

A good place to start to change old ways is making a commitment to your self-improvement!

Awareness of specific personal goals is the first step towards success. A type of structure, support and consistency are what ADD teens need, and where I started with Sara. With my insight, she was able to eliminate a lot of stress.

Plan *and* Schedule Efficiently

A day planner can be used to manage goals not time. A student may use the school planner that some schools give to students, but a student may also want to buy his own daily planner with a particular format. I recommend you get one with two pages to every day with time slots one half hour apart. This is what I suggest:

- The time for homework, tests, projects, appointments and obligations go in the appropriate time slot, in ink.

- On a piece of scrap paper, list your daily or weekly goals, then prioritize and pencil them in the appropriate time slots in order of importance or deadline.

- Use lined 3x4 sticky notes and write the following titles in small lettering in the space at the top: **To Go, To Do, To Buy, To Get,** and **To Call**. Specific items fill the lines of the sticky note.

- Place the sticky notes on top of the daily notes side of your daily planner.

- Check off things as you do them.

- Continue this procedure daily, caring over what you didn't accomplish to the next day.

Investigate computer software.

Many people find computer programs for planning and time management very beneficial. Making lists and checking off items as they are done is an excellent strategy. Some watches have enough memory to download time management information from or into your computer.

Stick with what works

Once you find a planning system that works for you, make sure to continue to use it even though you may start to feel like you don't need it if it's working, continue to use it, making refinements as you grow. Never give up a good thing!

Use a timer, or watch with an alarm, to stay on schedule

It may be useful to set time limits and alarms to keep on track. Be realistic about the amount of time it takes to complete each task. If you never have enough time, you may just be underestimating how long it takes.

Determine the value of the task to be done. If something is valuable enough to you, it is easier to keep trying to find a way to get it done.

Plan the night before.

Leave plenty of extra time for repeating a task, getting lost, or what ever may come up unexpectedly.

Write down your plans and structure the activities in logical order, so one task naturally leads into the next task. Writing down activities allows for you to see where you may group related activities to save time.

Example: By looking at your plans in writing you may decide it makes better sense to drop off the dry-cleaning on the way home from work instead of making two separate trips at different times of the day.

Establish priorities.

Making a list helps to see what needs to be done first.

Set realistic expectations.

- Once again, making a list may help to see there are not enough hours in the day to get everything done that you would like to accomplish.
- **Realize you can make "mistakes."** Allow them and forgive yourself. We all make mistakes. Need I say more?
- Delegate duties when possible to a friend, or family member.
- Focus on what you know you do best, and ask others to do the rest. If possible, get help for the things you're not good at. Ex. Tutor, coach

Manage goals, not time.

Write your goals for the week or day on a piece of paper prioritize them; put them in a day planner.

Here are some of the coaching strategies I suggest to my clients to help them to manage their time efficiently:

- Chunk it down, meaning breaking larger activities down into smaller steps. Think of the challenge before you as a chocolate bar scored in squares and each square is a task that needs to be done from beginning to end.

Do one task at a time, as you would savor each chunk of a chocolate bar, one chunk at a time; waiting to enjoy the next piece until you've completely enjoyed the first one, having gotten all the satisfaction out of it that you wanted. Mini deadlines and small rewards for finishing on time work well.

Example: Plan rewards at each step of the way. The reward could be fifteen minutes playing your favorite game on the computer.

- When sorting and handling paperwork, use the O.H.I.O. principle: Only Handle It Once! Put it in the proper pile or place as soon as you pick it up.
- Use a coach to help you plan, and to run your ideas by.

A coach is someone who is non-judgmental and has your interest in mind. She can review your ideas, negotiate with your parents, and encourage you, along with giving you support and suggestions without being too critical. A coach will encourage and root for you along your journey. She is someone to get feedback from and also is someone to call if you get off schedule or lose focus.

- Set reasonable limits without guilt about not trying hard enough. Be kind to yourself and keep your boundaries.
- Take care of your body, mind, and spirit. Give yourself the kind of emotional and physical nourishment you'll need to relieve any stress related anxiety.
- Always have a pad and pencil handy. Use it for recording ideas and things you need to remember. Always have a place to put those notes to refer to until done.
- Get in a routine and provide structure when you can. Routine usually works best.

- Schedule homework breaks. Figure out how long you can do your homework or study before getting distracted or frustrated. Take a 15-30 minute break.

- Schedule "down time" and fun time. This will help prevent becoming overwhelmed or burnt out.

- Make tedious tasks fun. Plan them as special events, and invite friends over to help you study, or do a project. Later you enjoy pizza and chat.

Time Management Summery

Teens with their coaches' assistance can create systems that they can refer back to. This will also help them to recognize their accomplishments when they start doing things routinely. Remember, you can have it all as long as you keep it simple and don't get stuck. Break goals, choices, and challenges into chunks or steps. Tackle it one step at a time until completion. Seeing that you can stick to a goal will empower you to stay on track and keep moving forward.

Times flies, but remember…you are the pilot.

8

Medication

People with ADD have conflicting information and thoughts regarding medicine as a treatment for their ADD. When asked my opinion, I tell parents and teens that medication is an increasingly important part of comprehensive mental and health treatment. Medications aren't an alternative to other forms of therapy. It goes hand in hand with coaching, therapy, and education. Teens should go to a doctor who specializes in medicating ADD and co-existing conditions that may accompany it.

Psychotherapy alone may be a failure in treatment, since ADD is a neurological condition and can't be "talked out." In order to modify adverse behavior, medication should be administered in conjunction with coaching, therapy, and education. Patients of all ages can benefit from medication. It can give a person with ADD full control over all of his inborn intellectual ability, perhaps the first time in his life. It is often surprising how fully controllable all the manifestations of what the condition are.

Stimulants are the treatment of choice for ADD. They must be taken regularly to be effective. A physician should monitor the medication. It is the responsibility of the parent, teen and coach to monitor it's the teen's behavior while on the stimulant medication. It is also crucial to monitor and report its effectiveness and side effects to the physician. Not everyone with ADD wants or needs to be medicated. At times the teens' parents or teens themselves do want medication to be an option. Some cases a teen can't take medication and other times they are still a few steps away from the comfort of the concept of meds. It is important to consult a physician who specializes in diagnosing and medicating ADD and its co-existing conditions.

In looking for a doctor who specializes in ADD, the parents and teen should decide on several questions that they want to ask.

The following are some appropriate questions

- How long have you been working with ADD?
- What percentage of your practice involves treating teens with ADD?
- How do you determine an ADD diagnosis?
- What is your treatment philosophy?
- How will we work together if I am your patient?

The doctor, coaches and other professionals must assess the particular symptoms in a person's life at that time, and evaluate the effects of these symptoms on the person's ability to perform in all aspects of his or her life. In my opinion, physicians help best when they take a conservative approach to drug treatments. With careful monitoring, unwanted side effects can be minimized and desired benefits maximized.

Characteristics frequently found in ADD students (No one must have all of them):

- They have a history of difficulty in school in both the learning and behavior areas
- They may have failed a grade or have been put back one or more years
- They may have difficulty and awkwardness in peer relationships into their teens
- They seem accident prone or clumsy
- They don't perform up to their apparent ability
- They frequently interrupt conversations
- They may have difficulty with coordination
- They respond poorly to discipline
- They are emotionally sensitive
- They have a tolerance to pain
- They have difficulty getting started, especially in the morning
- They find it difficult to get to sleep at night and get up in the morning

- They often are "violent" sleepers or bed-wetters, and often have sleep-walking or sleep talking in their history
- They have poor organizational skills
- They seek high-intensity highly stimulating environments
- They are very inactive or passive

Many teens have issues to be dealt with coaches and/or therapists due to their ADD and how it has affected their life. Teens consistently have been told they need to try harder from both their teachers and parents. Brain imaging studies by Dr. Daniel Amen have shown that the pre-frontal cortex of the brain actually "shuts down when they try harder." No wonder that a teen often complains that his mind goes blank when he takes an exam.

Regardless of age, medications can be used to give the person full control over all of his or her inborn, intellectual ability, perhaps for the first time in his life. If teens have a chemical problem, the problem is most effectively treated with a chemical solution.

As a coach, I proceed with the belief that the challenges I observe are controllable by proper medication, fully dosed in the most effective manner. It is often surprising how completely controllable all the manifestations of the condition are.

Many patients have co-morbid conditions. It is not uncommon to have ADD in combination with other disorders, such as anxiety, depression, learning disabilities, obsessive compulsive disorder, psychosis, and bipolar. A knowledgeable physician will be able to diagnose and treat the ADD and co-morbid conditions at the same time.

It is appropriate for a coach to ask what medications her clients are on and why they are on them. The coach should be familiar with medications in order to be able to monitor clients and advise them to make an appointment with their psychiatrist or neurologist if they are having any difficulties with their medications. It is also appropriate to offer to speak with a client's doctor or to request that a client get a second opinion if the doctor is unresponsive. A coach can help clients to communicate their requests and concerns to their parents and doctors. Some coaches will request signed permission to speak to their client's doctors and some doctors insist on them.

Jennifer

Jennifer, 16, has been seeing a coach for six months. In the sixth month, her coach noticed changes in her behavior and attitude that worried her, so she called a phone conference with Jennifer's parents.

Jennifer's parents informed her coach that Jennifer was not as motivated, spent a great deal of time listening to heavy metal music, was cutting school, failing math and history, and that her behavior was not consistent.

Jennifer's coach suggested first that they make an appointment with Jennifer's prescribing doctor. Her medications may need adjustment, the coach explained, or she may be forgetting to take them. She may also be experimenting with drugs and may need to be tested.

The coach's next suggestion was for Jennifer to begin work with a therapist. Jennifer's parents agreed with the wisdom of the coach's suggestions and thanked her for the consultation.

The coach followed up with Jennifer to make sure she understood that her coach was "standing for "Jennifer's success and sees her recent behavior as a sign of trouble ahead.

After some discussion, Jennifer admits that she has been having trouble and that she feels better to know that her coach is looking out for her. She agreed to talk to a therapist.

Her medication was adjusted after seeing her doctor, and she started using a watch alarm to remind her when to take her medication.

Three months later Jennifer was doing much better in all aspects of her life.

Medication Summary

Medication, therapy, coaching and educating oneself about ADD is the recommended approach to treatment. Some teens may need medication while others may not. A psychiatrist or neurologist specializing in ADD can make the recommendations as to which medications to take, are there co-existing conditions and whether or not to go the medication route. Coaches can ask questions to monitor the teen while taking medication in between doctor visits.

9

Education, the Law, and your ADD Child

As interest and awareness about Attention Deficit Hyperactivity Disorder grows, parents are also becoming educated about how to get the necessary help for their AD/HD child through the school system.

The Individual with Disabilities Act [IDEA] requires educators to classify ADD as a disability and to carefully plan for each child, using an Individual Educational Plan [I.E.P.]. This I.E.P. is a comprehensive plan of action for the school to follow in delivering services to the student. Teachers can play an important role in providing help for the ADHD students. A parent who believes that his/her child would benefit if he were classified as "learning disabled" should go through the process and investigate the various types of services available on both state and local levels.

Initially, many ADHD teens resist being evaluated for fear of being perceived as "different" by their peers. Parents should allow their teens to express their anger, sending them to counseling or getting them a coach if necessary, but still follow through with the evaluation process. Allowing the teen to play a part in the decision-making will help reduce his anger and make him more interested and less fearful. They deserve a chance to show up brilliantly.

The Law and your School System

The guarantee of a free public education is one of the most important rights as a citizen residing in the United States. There are laws to further protect the rights of children who have learning disabilities and/or who are disabled. An education that is appropriate to their needs is guaranteed by our nation to be accessible to children with Attention-Deficit/Hyperactivity Disorder [AD/HD].

There are two federal laws that guarantee the rights of a child with AD/HD to a free appropriate public education. These laws are Section 504 of the Rehabilitation Act of 1973 and the Individuals with Disabilities Education Act, IDEA, as amended in 1997.

Section 504 is a civil rights act. It prohibits public schools that receive federal funds from discriminating against children with disabilities. It states that students with AD/HD should be allowed to participate with other children in extracurricular and nonacademic activities.

The main difference between the two laws is that in order to be eligible for coverage under IDEA, a student must require special education services. With special education services, a student can get instruction in a special education classroom or may get instruction within a regular classroom (referred to as "inclusion").

Coverage under Section 504 is broader. A student can require either special education or related services. "Related Services" can refer to as the number of accommodations to the needs of a student with AD/HD.

Students with more severe difficulties are covered by IDEA and students with less severe challenges are usually covered by Section 504. If your child is eligible under both laws, you may have to decide which law better suits the needs of your child.

The Americans with Disabilities Act of 1990 (ADA) is a civil rights law. This law extends protection very similar to Section 504 to cover students with disabilities at non-religious private schools. ADA also prohibits discrimination in services, implementation of programs on the basis of disability.

One of the most important steps to get an education suited to your child's needs is to educate yourself on what you and your child are entitled to. A positive, persistent attitude and a lot of patience are very helpful also.

You will have to work through a system that includes programs defined, but not completely funded, by the United States government. Don't hesitate to ask your state and local school system, as well as your child's teachers, counselors, and special education department, to assist you in providing an education that is suited to your child. If needed, make sure an I.E.P. is in place. Do your homework: make sure you get enough information to understand what to include in your child's I.E.P.

Negotiating

Negotiating is an important tool to an AD/HD friendly education. Parents must be prepared to learn the laws as well as develop good communication skills with teachers and other school system personnel. Making the most out of your child's rights to a special education is a huge responsibility for parents or guardians.

Parents should be aware that there are evaluations and eligibility procedures, due process hearings, and Individualized Educational Plans (IEPs). This process can be frustrating and confusing. Some parents actually hire an education advocate to assist and guide them. An increasing number of ADD coaches specialize in parent advocacy with school systems.

Federal law requires schools and parents to write an I.E.P. together. The parents, teachers and school counselors are all involved in writing it. A good I.E.P. indicates the things a school can do that are most likely to help a student become more successful. It also provides a road map of the student's strengths and weaknesses.

Parents are responsible for monitoring their child's education to make sure the teacher follows the plan. Not all coaches offer this service, but if the coach is amenable, it is within the parent's rights to insist that the coach be included in I.E.P. discussions with the school.

The I.E.P. must be updated and re-written once a year. It can be amended at any time. Either the school or the parents can request that the I.E.P. be amended and both must participate. A teen's coach can make suggestions to the parent and write a letter to the school district for the student and his parents, even if the coach is not officially part of the process.

The following are some of the accommodations that an ADHD student may receive as part of his I.E.P.:

Instruction

- A note taker, or copy of teacher's notes
- A writer for student
- Use of computer to take notes and do assignments
- Buddy system with peer as tutor
- Use of tape recorder in class
- Reduce amount of class work

Homework

- Shorten assignments in individual subjects
- Extended time
- Permission to use Cliff Notes
- Duplicate set of textbooks and supplies at home
- Homework checklist in school and at home
- Scheduled breaks incorporated into homework
- Teach older student to use planner
- Put homework and tests due dates in planner
- Give frequent reminders about due dates
- Allow extra-credit assignments
- Develop and post routines on poster-board and hang in child's room
- Develop reward system for completed in-school work and homework

Grades

- Base grades on I.E.P. objectives
- Consider amount of improvement made by student to base grades
- Base grades on effort as well as achievement
- On classroom tests and homework assignments, circle incorrect answer and put correct answer

Communication

- Develop weekly/by-monthly progress reports
- Email parent/guardian if problem arises
- Schedule periodic parent/teacher meetings
- Parent should create a weekly journal
- Mail or email parents a schedule of homework assignments

Jericho

Jericho, one of my teen clients, is fifteen years old and was recently diagnosed with ADD. His parents hired me at a time when Jericho had hit rock bottom and was motivated to get help. He had been having many problems both at home and in school, and was very unhappy with himself and his life. After he was diagnosed and medicated, our coaching began. Jericho began to come to my office weekly very motivated about our coaching sessions. One by one we tackled his challenges and worked on finding his strengths. Over time, he has improved in many areas, including homework, grades, studying, organizational and time management skills. He is getting along better with his family, and a tutor is helping him with his weak subjects.

While coaching him, I noticed that Jericho was having difficulties in some areas that medication and coaching weren't helping. His mother came to the same conclusion and told me she wanted to have him evaluated to see if he could qualify for an I.E.P. She asked me to help and I wrote a letter informing the committee what I had observed about Jericho through our coaching sessions. I also suggested which modifications I believed would be necessary in order for Jericho to work up to his ability. Among these were assigning him a note taker and homework writer, reducing his amount of homework, giving him extra time to take tests and allowing him to take them in a separate room.

His mother came prepared to the meeting with his diagnosis, testing results, doctor's recommendations, etc. During the diagnostic team meeting, the administrator told Jericho's mother that they agreed that he should be eligible for the modifications. The team, along with Jericho's mother put an I.E.P. in place. They thanked her for Bringing my letter and told her it was informative and helpful to them in making their decision. These modifications, along with the coaching and medication, have made a great improvement in Jericho's self-esteem and performance. His attitude towards his family, school and life in general has improved. He has a lot of friends and is finally enjoying his teen years.

Steps that can help you get the most from the school system

Document the diagnosis

1. Have your child's psychiatrist, or neurologist write a letter with his recommendations.

2.   Study the laws.

3.   If your child is using a coach, have the coach write her recommendations.

4.   Consult with an advocate, attorney, or determine yourself if your child is eligible for special education services and request a written report.

Discuss your child's needs with the school as well as with the individual teachers.

1.   Arrange a meeting at your child's school with the child study team.

2.   Schedule a "due process hearing" if your child is judged ineligible for special education.

3.   If your child is eligible, put an I.E.P. in place.

4.   Work closely with your school system.

5.   Make sure you hear and comprehend what the system is saying to you.

6.   Make sure the educators involved are listening and hearing what you are saying.

7.   Do not challenge the teachers and school personnel. Challenge the school system to get what you feel is necessary.

Education and the Law Summary

Children with ADD are considered to have a disability and may qualify for several different services. Parents are responsible to making sure that their child is classified if necessary. Parents should become more knowledgeable about the accommodations that their children are entitled to. I suggest that parents read information from several sources or hire a special education advocate to advise them and to go with them to the IEP meetings.

10

The Future

ADD is a complex and unique disorder that has only recently begun to be more fully understood. Due to repeated failures, misunderstanding and mislabeling, children with ADD usually develop problems with their self-image and self-esteem. These children have been called dumb, stupid, lazy, stubborn and obnoxious. They often end up turning to drugs and alcohol as an escape. This can be prevented if society reaches out to this very intelligent, artistic, resourceful and creative group of people.

Coaching can be enormously beneficial to both teenagers and adults who have been diagnosed with any form of ADD as well as its co-existing conditions. For those suffering from ADD, the first step towards personal growth is for them to acknowledge that they have a neurobiological disability and seek help for it. With the help of medication, coaching, therapy and education, much can be accomplished.

Help and guidance makes teens more motivated, cooperative and productive at school and at home. It can also make them less aggressive and more self-confident. Certain ADD traits that were a challenge to teens as children may be highly valued as adults. For example, although the behavior of a teen with ADHD is not particularly valued in school, an adult who is able to work long hours and has high energy is an asset in the workplace.

Positive Features about AD/HD

A majority of teens with ADD go on to higher education. Many ADD and ADHD teens become adults who are **great** entrepreneurs, salespeople, business owners, artists and professionals. They can sometimes do three things simultaneously, which gives them a creative edge in the workplace. Once they are on medication and have had some coaching, these people find their niche and are usually very successful. Their determination and high energy help them achieve their goals.

ADD Gifts

Teens with ADD (and their parents) should keep in mind that there also advantages to having ADD, such as intuitiveness, creativity, high energy and enthusiasm. The disorder hasn't kept many people from great success in a variety of fields.

People with ADD are tuned into the world, and are very curious. They are always thinking of fresh and new ideas. They are often inventors and innovators, movers and doers. They have their own mold; and that is perfectly ok. It is better not to force them into a mold they don't fit.

Many ADD teens are extremely gifted, yet they sometimes do not recognize their gifts and talents until they work with a coach. As a rule, ADD teens are original, creative, intelligent, inventive, talented, daring, funny, sensitive and compassionate. Many famous and successful people have had AD/HD.

Special Qualities

Here are some of the special qualities common to people with AD/HD:

Creativity

People with ADD tend to be more creative than the average person. If creativity is nurtured, it can be enhanced. Many adults with ADD are talents authors, artists, actors or musicians.

Hyperactivity

Hyperactivity is usually thought of as an ADD challenge, but it can also be an advantage. The tendency toward hyperactivity has drawn many ADD teenagers into sports. They are usually good at whatever sports they choose.

By the time teens become adults, many have learned how to channel their hyperactivity. They have the extra energy to keep going and therefore they often accomplish more than others. Many highly successful adults have ADHD.

Writing Ability

An ADDer's natural creativity can be revealed in his ability to write. Most of the authors of ADD books have ADD themselves.

When I decided to write this book, for instance, I thought of my topic, wrote down names of chapters, and the ideas flowed onto the pages.

I tend to hyper-focus when I am doing something I enjoy. I wrote during every spare minute that I had. Writing quenches my thirst for self-expression and gives me the opportunity to share valuable insights and information with others.

Entrepreneurial Skills

ADD teens and adults make great entrepreneurs. They are not afraid to take risks and can follow through an idea.

The following client studies will provide a couple of fine examples of ADD entrepreneurship:

Brian

Brian needed to have a job while in high school. He worked as a mechanic's assistant and then worked in an auto parts store.

By the time he turned eighteen, Brian decided to start his own business. He began detailing cars. He told family and friends about his business and made business cards and flyers to distribute. Next, he went into auto repair shops. He currently has added a snow removal and landscape business and has a number of people working for him.

Brian just turned twenty-two.

Jennifer

Jennifer, another former client, started a pet-sitting business at age nineteen while she was still in college.

At twenty-two, after graduating from college, she got a position managing a large animal hospital practice. She maintains her pet-sitting business by employing a number of other people.

Inventiveness and Curiosity

Thomas Alva Edison has been referred to by many authors as learning disabled. Today, many experts think he may have had ADD.

As a student his handwriting was criticized, he was easily distracted and his teachers could not handle his behavior. People predicted he always would be a failure. He was taken out of school when he was in fifth grade to be home-schooled by his mother. The rest is history.

Children, teens and adults with ADHD are usually very curious. They tend to notice things that other people miss. They are not afraid to take a risk. They are always thinking of new ideas.

Teaching Potential

Teachers provide structure and have to be creative in order to teach their students well. ADDers make excellent teachers, particularly in the field of Special Education. Many ADDers were in Special Ed. Classes themselves as children. They know what worked for them and what bored them.

With their energy, creativity and determination working for them, many ADDers find that they can teach in their own style and do a great job. Time management is built into their day. With the help of a coach, they can work at providing structure for themselves and for their students.

Sam

Sam loved the sciences in high school. He hyper-focused in class and was an A student. He didn't do as well in his other classes, but he still maintained a 3.5 GPA. He thrived on the structure that school provided. In college, he majored in science. Eventually, he was back in his old high school as a teacher.

Taking Advantage of the Advantages

It may take working with a coach for a teen to realize what his or her gifts and talents are. If their abilities are in demand, they can become quite successful as adults. Yes, teens with ADD have to overcome many struggles in school and in their daily lives, but on their weakness and turning them into opportunities is something they can accomplish with help.

Parents, educators, and anyone who hopes to work successfully with ADD teens, should always look for something good to say to them.

A parent, teacher or coach can start by asking the teen to write down five things he is good at. The adult can do the same thing so they can compare answers. Together, they may also be able to think of other good qualities and achievements to add to the list.

A coach can also suggest to a teen to start a journal and to add to it every day. In this way, even small improvements will be noted.

Criticism can be expressed in a positive, rather than a negative way. For example, instead of saying, *"Don't shout out the answers in class!"* say "Isn't it great that you're so enthusiastic in class. I'm sure you'll learn to remember to raise your hand when you want to answer."

The Future Summary

Teens and their parents often worry about what the future will be for themselves and their ADD child. With all the resources there are today such as education, medication, therapy and coaching a teen's prognosis for success is very good. As mentioned above, the same symptoms and characteristics that the teen may have can be beneficial in there future once intervention is provided.

As a coach, I feel it is my duty to guide to work up to their full potential and keep them from falling through the cracks of our educational systems. Those who seek coaching bring with them a variety of backgrounds, challenges and gifts. Coaching can help them gain self-respect, confidence and encouragement. As a coach, helping and guiding clients is rewarding, gratifying, and fulfilling. I am committed to making a positive difference in their life, and I am dedicated to helping to educate professionals and the public about ADD so that early recognition and treatment will become routine.

11

What You Have Wanted to Ask

Millions of teenagers are discovering the reasons they can't perform like their classmates every day. Some are given logical, concise information about ADD and what to do about it, while others are not. I believe it is of critical importance to educate the public about attentional issues, coaching, learning modalities, as well as how and where to get help with this disorder.

Dr. Edward Hallowell has said many times that *"Coaching is the single most important tool for ADD self-management.*

I can tell you that the systems development approach used by ADD Coaches with training similar to mine works with individuals of all types, but is especially effective with ADDers.

Our ongoing goal is to shift expectations of failure to expectations of success. I personally champion my teen clients to develop a solid belief in their own abilities.

Questions and Answers

I hope I have covered most of your concerns in the previous pages of this book, but you might still have a few questions.

The remainder of this book is in Question/Answer format to give you some straight answers to questions I have heard before: the most common questions asked by ADDers as well as their families and teachers.

I hope these answers will be helpful to *you*.

General Information

Q: What causes ADD?

A: ADD is a neurological and biochemical disorder. Researchers believe that one of the causes of ADD is caused by a chemical imbalance in the brain, such as too much or too little dopamine, epinephrine, or serotonin. It is also believed that people with ADD do not have the right amount of neurotransmitters in the gaps between nerves in the brain.

What this means is that the brain's filtering and focusing areas are not operating adequately: there is difficulty sorting out incoming stimuli. The strongest stimulus (a striking color, movement, noise) grabs the person's attention. These results in a "lock" on consistency in functioning: hyperactivity (ADHD), hypoactivity (ADD) (involuntary daydreaming) or a mixture of the two.

Q: Why is ADD so common?

A: ADD has always been around, but it has been under-diagnosed in most cases. An estimated 8 million to 15 million people have ADD. Today there are millions of children and adults who have ADD but have never been diagnosed.

Q: Is ADD different in boys and girls?

A: Females are more likely to seem distracted or inattentive (ADD). Males are more prone to hyperactivity (ADHD): they are easier to diagnose because of their behavior. In fact, three times as many males are diagnosed than females. It is likely that there are many undiagnosed females.

Q: What are some common co-existing disorders with ADD?

A: Depression, anxiety, learning disorders, substance abuse, behavioral disorders, sleep disorders, conduct disorders, Toilettes Syndrome, Asperser's Syndrome, and mood disorders, Bipolar, Obsessive Compulsive Disorder

Q: Why does ADD make people seem "scattered" and less attentive?

A: The brain is having trouble sorting out incoming stimuli, jumping from one thing to another, so it is hard to focus one's thoughts on one thing at a time. The ADDer appears scattered and inattentive. Even speech may be impaired, with words coming out wrong. Yet if one is very interested in what one is doing or learning, he or she can "hyper-focus." This means he/she can spend hours focused on one activity and even lose track of time because they are so engrossed!

Q: Is someone with ADD more likely to use illegal drugs?

A: Not necessarily, but undiagnosed, untreated ADD can lead to extreme anxiety that people may try to alleviate with drugs. It is also possible that people with

ADD have a tendency toward addictive behaviors including substance abuse, overeating, gambling, compulsive shopping and overworking.

Q: What is the relationship between undiagnosed ADD and drug use?

A: Dr. Edward Khantzian, a psychoanalyst and specialist in the field of substance abuse came up with a "self-medication" hypothesis. Khantzian proposes the idea that people use drugs to treat subconscious bad feelings. The use of cocaine, marijuana,

Alcohol and tobacco is a kind of self-prescribed medication for whatever ails them emotionally. The drug then creates its own emotional and physical problems. For example, one might subconsciously use marijuana to alleviate feelings of low self-esteem, or use alcohol to treat depression (even though alcohol ultimately causes depression).

How is this concept applied to people with undiagnosed ADD? Many people who have ADD, but don't know it, feel bad about themselves. They feel they are different from other people, but they don't know why. They may become depressed, anxious, agitated, distracted, or unfocused, but they cannot recognize how they feel. These unrecognized and untreated feelings can lead to substance abuse as an attempt to "self-medicate."

Q: Do drugs and stimulants affect someone with ADD in a different way than they affect someone without ADD?

A: Generally, yes. Cocaine is an example of a class of drugs we call psycho-stimulants (or stimulants). Two standard medications used to treat ADD, Adderall and Ritalin, are also example of stimulants. People with ADD feel focused when they take stimulants, where many people *without* ADD feel a rush of unfocused energy (speed).

Even with an illegal stimulant like cocaine, an ADDer will feel focused in a similar way they feel when they use Adderall or Ritalin: clear-headed and able to pay attention. However, this feeling lasts only a short time. When they come off cocaine, they feel worse than when they were not taking it. The desire to feel good again can put them into a cycle of chronic cocaine use and can lead to addiction.

Similarly, alcohol tends to quiet the "internal noise" that trouble some ADD teens and adults. In the short term, alcohol use reduces the anxiety commonly associated with ADD. Alcohol is a depressant, however, and in the long run, anxiety increases from the daily cycle of withdrawal associated with chronic alcohol abuse.

Marijuana also tends to quiet the noise inside and help the ADD user "chill out." This, too, has only a short-term effect, and repeated use of marijuana as an anti-anxiety agent results in a decrease in motivation.

Q: How is the treatment for addictions different for someone with ADD?

A: The ADD must be treated as well as the addiction. When the ADD is treated, it is much less likely that the person will go back to drug abuse. Hopefully, he will be put on the right medications for the ADD and other co-existing conditions he may have. He should be closely monitored by his psychiatrist, especially while the medication levels are adjusted to the correct dosage for his optimal functioning capacity.

The prescription medication for ADD should do a much better job of helping him cope with the challenges of ADD than the illegal drugs. With help, supervision, and coaching, he can remain drug-free.

The following is the experience of one of my clients.

Rob

"Rob," age 18, is in counseling for his drug problem. He stopped taking cocaine a year ago.

Ten months ago, he was diagnosed with ADD.

His psychiatrist took a while to find the right combination of medications for him, but ultimately put him on one medication for ADD and two medications for anxiety and depression. He visits his psychiatrist once a month to monitor his medications and functioning.

When his ADD was discovered, both his prescribing doctor and his therapist recommended that he work with an ADD coach. That is when he was referred to me.

Rob has also added attendance at AA meetings, although he told me that *he hasn't felt an urge to take cocaine since he started his prescription medications.*

Together we have been working on overcoming his personal and academic challenges, and achieving his goals for a fulfilling life.

It has been nine months since I started coaching Rob. So far, he is drug-free and doing very well. He is ambitious and determined to succeed.

Questions from parents or teachers of ADDers:

Q: Is a child born with ADD?

A: Yes. It is believed to be a genetic chemical imbalance.

Q: Are people with ADD less likely to succeed in life?

A: No, there are many famous and successful people who have ADD—doctors, attorneys, authors, teachers, artists, salespeople and scientists. If evaluated, many of the most creative people in the world would probably be found to have some form of ADD. People with ADD are usually gifted, artistic, athletic, talented and/or creative.

Researchers now believe that Thomas Edison, among other highly creative people, probably had ADD. Drs. Edward Hallowell and John Ratey are well known adult/child psychiatrists specializing in ADD. They believe that the people who explored and founded this country were the sort of people who couldn't sit still, who were willing to take risks and who were in search of new and exciting things—the clear characteristics of ADD! The only problem is that often it takes time for most people to realize their talents and how to use them.

Q: In what ways can other people help those who have ADD?

A: The first and best way to help is for non-ADDers to learn about ADD themselves. Unless they understand this unique disorder, it will be hard to truly help someone who has it. Of course, always treat them (and everyone) with respect.

The next step would be to ask to person with ADD how you can be of help. Encourage the Adder not to be afraid to ask for whatever kind of help is needed. Break down the particular needs of the Adder into categories, and then outline the steps it would take to find solutions or systems that would help. If you are not able to be of help, get someone who can.

Q: Should a coach who does not specialize in ADD coach an ADD client?

A: Not really. A generic coach hasn't been trained about ADD symptoms and challenges. He or she would not be familiar with ADD treatments and medication. It is more effective to have someone specifically trained to deal with ADD coach ADD clients

Q: Why haven't I heard of ADD coaching before?

A: ADD coaching has been in existence for around ten years and has not been well publicized. Magazine articles are occasionally written about it, but most people learn of ADD coaching through word of mouth, the Internet, or in some books about ADD.

Q: Why do parents have to be an advocate for their ADD child?

A: If the parent is not an advocate, no one else will be. The school system will do little for your child unless you make requests. Find out what you child is entitled to legally in your school district. Ask your child's doctor, teachers (and your child!) what is needed in order for your ADD child to have an enriched, challenging and successful school career.

Q: If a boy or girl is not disruptive in class, but simply daydreams when the teacher is talking, is it likely he or she has ADD?

A: Of course, some children daydream now and then in class, and it does not mean that they have ADD. But if the daydreaming is persistent, a diagnosis may be in order. Years ago, children of this kind were not diagnosed as having ADD. Teachers just thought that daydreamers were just not very bright, and many of them "fell between the cracks" of the educational system. We now know that most of these children probably have inattentive ADD. The same stimulant medication that works for ADHD usually helps ADD. With the medication, the student can focus on what the teacher is saying and concentrate on schoolwork appropriately.

Q: What are the common academic problems linked to ADD or ADHD?

A: Many ADD, ADHD students have slow processing speed and impaired working memory. These skills are critical for working math problems and writing essays.

With word problems, for instance, the student must hold several numbers and questions in mind while deciding how to work the problem. To find the correct math rule to use for the problem, he must delve into long-term memory. He must hold several facts in mind as he applies the rules and shifts information back and forth between working and short-term memory.

Written expression is the most frequent learning problem among students with ADD or ADHD. Consequently, writing essays, answering questions on tests, doing written homework or drafting book reports are often extremely challenging for these students. Processing all the information needed for the essay, remembering what to write down, organizing the material into logical sequence, editing and correcting errors can feel like overwhelming tasks.

Q: Why does an ADD child blurt out answers to the teacher's questions before anyone else has a chance to raise his or her hand?

A: The child has anxieties about following through with action. She is afraid she will forget the answer by the time she raises her hand and the teacher calls on her. The teacher or coach should suggest that the child keep a pad in front of her and write down the answer when it comes to her. Then she can raise her hand like everybody else and wait to be called on.

Q: Does ADD affect a teen's social skills?

A: Absolutely. Teens with ADD tend to be lacking in social skills. There were a lot of social skills their peers acquired as they were growing up that missed the attention of the Adder. This explains their immature social behavior. A coach can point out to them, in a non-threatening way, what behavior is expected and is acceptable. Once they are on medication as well, they are more aware of important social skills and they usually improve. As a result, their peers begin to see them in a better light and they find it easier to make friends (which increase their self-esteem). They tend to be more socially sure of themselves as their self-esteem improves.

Q: Is a reward system a good idea for my ADD child?

A: Many times, it is a great idea. Keep a few things in mind before you start: Agree on the reward ahead of time. What is fair and equitable? Exactly what will have to be achieved in order to receive the reward?

Then, keep track of progress and successes, using a chart if possible. Follow through consistently. The reward should be something the child would particularly enjoy: stickers for her sticker collection; a special outing one-on-one with the parent; a CD; tickets to a special event or concert.

Q: How can I help my teen establish routines?

A: If your teen has a coach, suggest that the coach help him or her prioritize the routines needed and then work on them one at a time in a systems development manner. (See below.) If your teen does not have a coach, you can discuss the routines needed and which are most important. Suggest a morning routine (to get ready for school), an after-school routine to implement doing homework and/or household chores, and an evening routine for getting ready for bed and planning the next day. You can use the systems development techniques described below.

Q: What is "systems development?"

A: This is a process of accomplishing a chore, task or goal by breaking it down into steps and tackling it one step at a time. You create a system by listing the steps you have to take in sequence. Then you proceed.

Questions from ADDers themselves

Q: Why do I have trouble staying mentally focused?

A: Too many things are grabbing your attention at the same time. You see a red sweater, hear a door slam, think about your after-school plans, and stare out the window simultaneously.

Focusing is **selective**: sometimes you can retain focus and other times you can't.

With ADD, attention is better termed "the process of attending." Attending is a three-part process:

8. Focusing on the intended subject

9. Maintaining the focus

10. Shifting or changing focus at will (rather than involuntarily., as when distracted)

In addition to medication prescribed by your doctor, your coach can give you tools to sharpen your awareness and help you focus. These tools can be as simple as kinesthetic tactics like doodling or quietly squeezing a crunch ball. Your coach will help you find what works for you.

Q: Why do doctors and teachers want me to take medication for my ADD?

A: The right medication or combination of medications, and the correct dosage (once they have been ascertained) can make a remarkable difference in your life because they make a remarkable difference in your ability to function.

Things that was once extremely difficult for you will become much easier. You notice more things and you will better relate to your environment. Your processing of information will be better. The list goes on: all your ADD symptoms will come under better control.

Once you are on the right meds, evaluate the change after three months and you will notice yourself that medication is well worth the trouble of taking it.

Think of it this way: your brain is lacking an adequate amount of something and the medication supplies what is lacking. Meds are important to me and to all of my clients.

Q: Will I overcome ADD when I am older?

A: You may be able to take less medication as an adult, if you have developed strategies and systems when you were younger. It also depends on how severe the ADD is, how well you function and what your functioning needs are, which is determined to a large degree by the kind of life you choose to live.

Q: Why would I need a coach to help me cope with ADD?

A: As my book illustrates, an ADD coach partners with you, yet is someone you have to answer to: a coach keeps you accountable for what you say you are going to do.

A coach gets you on track, makes sure you stay on track, helps you overcome your challenges and achieve your goals. If you are committed to personal growth and want to see progress, a coach is for you.

Q: How does coaching compare to therapy? Can one replace the other, or do I need both?

A: In therapy, you are dealing with psychological issues from the past to the present. You will talk a good deal about your feelings.

Coaching is more action oriented. It teaches you to take action to move forward toward achieving change and personal growth. Therapy and coaching go hand in hand. You must work on resolving personal issues so you can take action.

Q: How long will I need coaching?

A: The length of time varies from individual to individual. On average, teenagers benefit most from one to three years of coaching. Continue the coaching for as long as you feel you are still learning, growing and accomplishing goals through it. Adults tend to use coaching for an average of two years. Unfortunately, financial concerns may cause you to curtail coaching, as it is not usually covered by insurance.

Q: Should I tell my friends I have ADD?

A: It isn't necessary, but you can tell your close friends if you want to. Be prepared to answer questions about ADD, such as *"What is ADD?"* and *"How did you get it?"*

Also, be prepared for the possibility that they may not keep your secret. If you have good self-esteem, you will be fine even if your ADD becomes publicly known. If not, you might want to wait until your self-esteem improves before you confide to your friends about your ADD.

Q: Should I tell my school that I have ADD?

A: Yes, your parents or guardian should tell your school that you have ADD. They will need a note from your doctor. By informing the Special Education department, you will be eligible for special services (such as an IEP—Individual Education Plan) if needed. How ADD interferes with your learning will determine what services you should seek. Know that these services are available to you.

Q: Isn't Special Education for kids who are stupid?

A: No—that is a myth. Many Special Education students are very bright, but they learn better with the special benefits and techniques available through this type of program such as smaller class size, more individual attention and multimodal teaching. A lot of Special Education students are mainstreamed to regular classes for some subjects.

Q: What can a student do to become more organized?

A: Planning is the key to organization.

1. Learn how to use a daily planner.

2. Do your planning at night for the next day.

3. Plan times when you are going to do homework.

4. Plan break times.

5. Put school clothes out the night before.

6. But your schoolbooks and everything else you will need for school at the exit door at night, ready to take the next day.

7. Put activities for the week on a family calendar (or on your own personal calendar in a visible place in your room).

Q: What is hyper-focusing?

A: You hyper-focus when you concentrate very hard on something and you are able to block out irrelevant stimuli. Some people have to set an alarm clock to remind them to stop working at a particular time. ADDers who can do this are manipulating their hyper-focus to their advantage.

Q: What is rumination?

A: Rumination is the act of constantly worrying about negative thoughts. Pay attention to the thoughts you create! Ruminating can keep you from enjoying life.

Q: What is impulsivity?

A: Impulsivity is the inability to regulate a sudden mental urge, resulting in impetuous action. In other words, it is acting before you think. Impulsivity is common in many ADDers, so don't think you are the only one coping with this problem.

Q: In school, I am easily distracted by other people around me, as well as by people coming into or going out of the room. I then have a hard time recapturing what I was learning. What can I do?

A: Choose a seat away from the doorway and windows (and not facing them) and close to the teacher. Near the blackboard is often a good location. (It might also help you to doodle or hold a squeeze ball to help you focus.) Try to jot down what you were doing or learning about when you were distracted

Q: I am forgetful about daily activities and have difficulty retaining information. What can I do about it?

A: Ask your coach to teach you to use tools such as daily planners, lists, erasable pens, timers and steno pads. He or she can also suggest routines and systems that will help you remember.

Here are some memory tips you can use right now. To better understand and remember information, think in terms of examples: form visual pictures in your mind; give yourself auditory cues. Repeating information to yourself is also helpful.

Q: The student next to me talks all the time and clowns around. I can hardly hear the teacher. What can I do about it?

A: If you have already tried to ask the student to quiet down and it has not helped, ask the teacher to change your seat. Although that student may have undiagnosed ADD and isn't really doing it on purpose, being distracted by this person can put a lot of stress on you.

Q: I can't concentrate when my teacher asks me (or other students) to read out loud. What can I do about this?

A: If the teacher plans to have a story, or poem read aloud in class, he or she should tell you the night before. This way, you will have the chance to read the material beforehand to be able to concentrate on it.

Q: I have a habit of interrupting others who are speaking. To be honest, I talk first and think later. How can I overcome this need to interrupt?

A: Interrupting others in conversation is tactless and won't earn you any friendships. Carry a little pad and a pen and write down what you want to say, so you won't forget it. Ask your coach or parent to teach you when it is polite to enter a conversation, (such as at a pause). You will need to practice thinking first, before you speak.

Q: Can you give me a brief list of some of the things I can do to help myself?

A: Ask for help when you need it, delegate jobs you are not good at, convert negative thinking into positive, simplify your life, learn study skills, get a homework buddy, and don't limit your expectations.

Q: Can you give me a simple system for homework?

A: In school:

1. Copy assignments down in a homework pad.

2. Gather all the materials you will need and bring them home.

Then, at home:

1. Decide what time you will do your homework and find a quiet place to work in.

2. Do the homework assignment you wrote down in your pad. Check that it is complete and accurate before you consider it finished.

3. Put the finished homework in your book bag and put the book bag near the door.

4. Take your homework back to school.

Q: What strategy can I use to help overcome my difficulty with writing?

A: Taking notes:

1. Take notes of just a few words at a time as you read or listen as someone reads material to you.

2. If necessary, have someone else take notes as you just listen.

3. Afterward, rewrite notes that are in sentence fragments into full sentences.

4. Arrange the sentences in proper order.

Writing stories or school reports:

1. Write down the subject.

2. List anything that comes to mind about the subject.

3. Eliminate topics on your list that are not directly on the subject.

4. Put topics in sequence, arranging them in logical order.

5. Use reference material (if appropriate).

6. Make an outline.

7. Write the outline in sentences.

8. Put sentences into paragraphs, using an opening sentence and a closing sentence on each paragraph.

Q: I always move around while I am studying (which my parents and teachers tell me not to do). I get good grades, so is there any reason not to keep moving?

A: You are probably a kinesthetic learner, so moving around actually helps you concentrate. By moving while you study, you process information better. Explain this to your parents and teachers, and point out that your grades prove that you do better with activity than by sitting still while you study.

Q: When I have a large project to do, I tend to start it and stop it. How do I get myself back to it?

A: It's OK to work on a project at different intervals. To make sure you will come back to it, do this:

Before you stop, write notes on stickers telling you where you left off and what you need to do next. Place the stickers on the parts of the project you need to work on next.

Try to have a designated area you can work in, so you can leave your project there. You will find that the more you start and stop and go back to it, the easier it will become to do this in the future.

Q: What is standing in the way of my completing my project?

A: It could be perfectionism. If it doesn't look perfect to you, it isn't worth completing. This is your illusion; to someone else your project could look great.

Are you a perfectionist? Change negative self-talk into positive self-encouragement.

Q: How do I let go of perfectionism?

A: You need to do a lot of positive "self-talk" and believe what you are saying! Tell yourself that it's OK not to be perfect—the world isn't perfect! Just start what you are going to do and get to the core value and main benefit of it. Tell yourself that it's wonderful to be an individual and that you can create something as individual as you are.

Q: What can I do to make sure I complete tasks?

A: There are a number of things that will help:

1. Plan to spend enough time for the task.

2. Break large projects into smaller ones.

3. Take planned breaks.

4. If frustration sets in, do something else for a while; exercise, take deep breaths or meditate.

5. If interrupted while working, write down what you were doing before going off the subject. Then return to the task after the break.

Q: Why am I always late?

A: There could be many reasons for consistent lateness. Poor time management, disorganization, and lack of awareness of how long it takes to do something—all lead to the habit of being late. You can change your behavior once you can pinpoint what causes your lateness.

Here are a few things that will help you keep on track (and also help you be on time):

-   A palm pilot,
-   A pulsating (vibrating) watch with 15-minute reminders,
-   Daily check-in calls.

Q: I'm always losing things, especially my keys. What can I do to remember where I put things?

A: Here's a good tip:

Always keep important things, like keys, in the same place. In this case, have a basket or a hook near the exit door and always put your keys there. The trick is to remember to put them there as soon as you walk in the door! Make this a habit and you'll spend a lot less time looking for things.

Q: Everyone tells me I should learn to set priorities. Why is that so important?

A: When you have many things to do, you have to decide in what order to do them. We put them in order of importance and time-sensitivity. What has to be done right now—go to school or call your friend? What has to be done next—go to class or go to the cafeteria? Is a doctor's appointment more important than picking up a new CD? These may seem like simple decisions, but they become more complex as life goes on.

We must learn how to prioritize because it affects our whole life.

To prioritize a list of tasks, simply list them in whatever order you think of them. Then put a number next to each one, ranking it in importance. You will instantly know what to do first, second, etc.

Q: How can I feel better about myself?

A: Instead of worrying about what you can't do, sit down (right now!) and write a list of things that you have accomplished in your lifetime. Each day, go back and add to the list. You may want to put the list on a bulletin board where you can easily see it and reread it. Leave enough room on the board for several sheets of paper!

Finale

ADD is a very complex and unique disorder. The genetic research and research using functional brain scans are enabling neuroscientists to better understand the ADD brain. The research is an ongoing process, which benefits millions of teen and adult ADDers by helping to explain ADD challenges. Once teens have an ADD foundation and understand how it affects them they experience a sense of relief. No wonder they have had so much difficulty with their life challenges. Best of all, it is not their fault and there is help available.

I coach teens from my heart, soul and gut. It is rare that I turn a teenager away when they come to me, sometimes as a last resort. I try every tool I know to get through to them, to have them respect me as I respect them and to win their trust. It may take a lot of time and energy but the rewards are worth it.

Supportive coaches, parents, teachers, educators, and bosses are extremely important in turning failure into success. Teens need structure, clear rules, and expectations from the adults who work with them. The adults need clear heads and loving hearts to help them know when and how to modify the rules.

Encourage, praise, be a cheerleader and you will be successful with any teen. Too often teens are reminded of what they can't do and seldom reminded of what they can. When a teen finally does something right, they are rarely praised enough to balance the feedback.

A teacher who welcomes individuality and creativity into her classroom and into her assignments is likely to have success with ADD teens. Of course, that also depends if a doctor is treating the teen, if the teen is on medication that works and if the teen has a coach.

ADD Coaches are fortunate that motivated teens are the ones who participate in coaching, with clearly supportive parents, since they are usually the ones paying the coach's fee. Teens in coaching are often receiving additional support from therapists, tutors, and books along with their families.

Coaching can be extremely beneficial to teenagers as well as adults, following a diagnosis of any form of ADD, including one that includes co-existing conditions. It is possible for a teen to benefit tremendously from the help of a coach, but how quickly a teen progresses is primarily up to them.

The first step toward personal growth is for them to acknowledge to themselves that they have a disability. Hopefully they have been informed that there is help for them through medication, coaching, therapy, and education. If a teen wants help and guidance, they are usually very coach able. Once they work with a coach, teens usually begin to feel better about them.

As I coach teens I teach them many things: study skills, time management, social skills, stress-management, anger managements and how to overcome the ADD challenges. We also work together to identify their gifts and achieve their goals in a systems development manner.

Help and guidance make teens more motivated, more accommodating, more productive in school, less aggressive, promoting higher self-esteem. Each teenager's greatest room for growth is the area of his greatest strengths. Each teen's talents are enduring and unique.

Certain ADD behaviors that were a challenge to teens as children may be highly valued as adults. For example, AD/HD is not particularly valued in school. As an adult being able to work long hours and have high energy is valued at the office, or as a physician, artist, etc.

Many ADD and ADHD adults are great entrepreneurs, sales people, business owners, artists, and professionals. They can sometimes do three-things simultaneously once they are on medication and have had some coaching. Once teens find their niche, they are usually great at it. Their determination and high energy helps them achieve their goals.

For some teens with ADD or ADHD it is truly a disability. Some teens have difficulties doing or completing a task. We must remember that ADD affects each individual differently. Some teens are on medication and others are not. We should respect all people, regardless of their disabilities.

I will coach any individual who has the determination to achieve their goals and have the courage to take the action needed in order to live the life they envision.

My clients bring with them very interesting backgrounds, challenges, and gifts. I give them the respect, belief, self-esteem, confidence, encouragement, and a little nudge. They need to take on the responsibility of changing their life from just getting by, to becoming successful, productive individuals.

As a coach, I go an extra mile for my students. A majority of them go on to higher education and become successful in a wide range of careers. I strive to guide clients as they reach their optimum functioning. Helping and guiding my clients is rewarding, gratifying, and fulfilling. I am committed to making a positive difference in their life. I am dedicated to help educate professionals and the public about ADD so that early recognition and treatment become routine.

For a teenager to have AD/HD is not a curse. Finding what works to bring out the gifts and overcome the challenges is a challenge well worth investing time and energy in. Respect teens and their individuality and you will receive respect from them. Love them, praise them, embrace the passion and most important, do anything in your power to help them help themselves. As they mature, you will see these misconceived teens turn into responsible, capable adults. Who knows, maybe some of them will become famous like their forefathers!

Appendix 1

References

There are many good sources of information on AD/HD. The following lists are some of the ones that shaped my thinking as I wrote the book.

Amen, Daniel G. (2001) *Healing ADD*. G.P. Putnam & Sons.
Amen, Daniel G. (1998). *Change Your Brain Change Your Life*. Three Rivers Press, NY, NY
Amen, Daniel G. (2002) *Images into the Mind*, G.P. Putman's Sons, NY, NY

Annual Conferences of National ADD Organizations

ADDA—The National Attention Deficit Disorder Association
CH.A.D.D.—Children and Adults with Attention Deficit Disorder

Griffith-Haynie, Madelyn, CTP, CMC, MCC: the A.C.T. Program, comprehensive ADD Coach Training from ADDCoach.com and The Optimal Functioning Institute™ [OFI]-and materials from her *A.C.T. Manual* (ver. 1 ©1994)

Hallowell, Edward M., MD and **Ratey, John J.,** MD (1994) *Driven to Distraction*, Touchstone Publisher, NY, NY. Pgs. 201, 151-194, 215-268, 225-235.
Hallowell, Edward M. MD and Ratey, John J., MD (1994). *Answers to Distraction*, Touchstone Publisher, NY, NY.

Kelly, Kate and **Ramundo, Peggy** (1996). *You Mean I'm not Lazy, Stupid or Crazy?!* Fireside, NY, NY.

Mooney, Jonathan and **Cole David (2000***). Learning Outside the Lines*, Fireside & Colephen, NY, NY.

Quinn, Patricia O., MD (1994) *ADD and the College Student,* Imagination Press, NY, NY.

Quinn, Patricia O., MD; **Ratey, Nancy A.,** Ed.M., MCC; **Maitland, Theresa L,** Ph.D., (2000) *Coaching College Students with ADHD,* Advantage Books.

Sosin, David and Myra (1996*) Professional's Guide to Attention Deficit Disorder,* Teachers Created Materials, Inc.

The New York Education Department, the Office of Special Education Services (OSES), *A Parents Guide to Special Education for Children Ages 5–21*

Appendix 2

Resources

Professional Organizations to contact for information about ADD

Attention Deficit Disorder

ADDA—National Attention Deficit Disorder Association: www.add.org
CH.A.D.D.—Children and Adults with Attention Deficit Disorder: www.chadd.org
NCGIADD—National Center for Gender Issues and ADHD, Director, Patricia O. Quinn, MD: www.ncgiadd.org
AD-IN—Attention Deficit Information Network—AD-IN www.addinfonetwork.com

Learning Disabilities

LDA—Learning Disabilities Association of America: www.ldanatl.org
National Center of Learning Disabilities—NCLD: www.neld.org
National Institute of Mental Health: www.nimh.nih.gov

Coaching

International Coach Federation—ICF: www.coachfederation.org
For Certification and Accreditation and Coach Referral
(A large majority of ICF coaches are not ADD-knowledgeable, so make sure you hire one who is)
ICF Certifications:
Associated Certified Coach—ACC
Coach Specific Training Hours: 60

Client Coaching Hours Experience:	250
Professional Certified Coach—PCC	
Coach Specific Training Hours:	125
Client Coaching Hours Experience:	750
Master Certified Coach—MCC	
Coach Specific Training Hours:	200
Client Coaching Hours Experience:	2500

ADD-specific Coach Training

ADDCoach.com™ and The Optimal Functioning Institute [OFI]
A.C.T. Program, Peer Coaching Curriculum,
Challenges Inventory Curriculum (with Certification & Licensing),
Founder: Madelyn Griffith-Haynie: www.addcoach.com
ADD Coach Academy-ACA
Director: David Giwerc www.addcoachacademy.com

Magazines and Newsletters with ADD Information

The following are the popular and informative magazines and newsletters on ADD. Visiting their web sites will be helpful, and is an easy way to subscribe.

Attention! Magazine, included with a membership to CHADD.—www.CHADD.org

ADDitude Magazine—www.ADDitude.com

Focus Magazine, comes with membership to ADDA.—www.ADD.org

American Academy of Child-Adolescent Psychiatry. Great website for parents—www.aacap.org

ADD ADHD Advances, E-mail Newsletter—www.addadhdadvances.com

ADDvance, E-mail Newsletter, a site dedicated to girls and women with ADD—www.ADDvance.com

About Attention Deficit Disorder, recent news about ADD.—www.add.about.com

All Kinds of Minds, E-mail Newsletter, information and resources about learning disabilities.—www.allkindsofminds.org

ADHD news, E-mail Newsletter, continually updated information about ADD.—www.ADHDnews.com

The Bipolar Child Website—www.bipolarchild.com

Obsessive Compulsive (OC) Foundation—www.ocfoundation.org

NAMI: National Mental Health Association—www.nmha.org

Support Group.com, a collection of electronic support group links—www.support-group.com

Appendix 3

About the Author

Joyce Walker, MCC, is a Master Certified Coach, an author and a freelance writer. .Joyce is one of the few coaches trained by a two year coach training program, OFI-ACT, specializing in ADD Coaching. She is based in Congers, New York.

Joyce received her Master Coach Certification through the International Coaching Federation [ICF] in 1999; the first time certification was available. She is also certified to coach individuals without ADD.

Joyce is founder of Crystal Clear Coaching and is in private practice for her AD/HD Coaching. Joyce works with teens and their parents. She is a life and professional coach who also coaches adults. Coaching is done in person or on the phone.

She is a member of many coaching organizations; including CHADD, ICF, ADDA, and the NCA. Joyce attends several national conferences yearly to keep current with the cutting age of research and developments in the ADD and coaching fields.

Appendix 4

Contacting the Author

I hope this book has been beneficial and will be inspiring to all who read it. I welcome your comments and will be delighted answer any questions or concerns.

For more information, feedback, comments, or coaching services, please contact me.

I can be reached by telephone at:

(845) 268-6473 or **(845) 641-1114**,

and by email at:

jwcoach@aol.com

http://www.crystalclearcoach.com

Make sure you remember to include your phone number.

I look forward to hearing from you!

Joyce Walker, MCC
August, 2005

978-0-595-37038-2
0-595-37038-1

Made in the USA
Lexington, KY
25 April 2011